INTRODUCTION TO INGRES

Margaret A. Zinky
Phoenix College

James W. Everett
Glendale Community College

Linda J. Hawbaker

PWS-KENT Publishing Company, Boston

PWS–KENT
Publishing Company

Sponsoring Editor: Jonathan Plant
Production Editor: Patricia Adams
Assistant Editor: Mary Thomas
Editorial Assistant: Heidi Greenman
Manufacturing Coordinator: Lisa M. Flanagan
Typesetter: Pine Tree Composition, Inc.
Interior and Cover Designer: Patricia Adams
Cover Printer: John P. Pow Company, Inc.
Printer/Binder: Maple-Vail Book Manufacturing Group

PWS-KENT Publishing Company is a division of Wadsworth, Inc.

Printed in the United States of America.

1 2 3 4 5 6 7 8—97 96 95 94 93 92

Library of Congress Cataloging-in-Publication Data

Zinky, Margaret
  Introduction to INGRES / Margaret A. Zinky, James W. Everett,
Linda J. Hawbaker.
    p. cm.
  Includes index.
  ISBN 0-534-92869-2
  1. Data base management. 2. INGRES (Computer system)
3. Relational data bases. I. Everett, James W. II. Hawbaker,
Linda J. III. Title.
QA76.9.D3Z56 1992
005.75′65—dc20   91-26812
                                                        CIP

PREFACE

This book is intended as an introduction to INGRES database tools. The book assumes that the user has had relatively little exposure to the tools, but is familiar with general database concepts. Although there is a brief discussion of databases in general in Chapter One of this book, there has been no attempt to make this a complete explanation of database software design or theory.

Following the introduction the book is divided into four parts. Part Two is intended for those who have had little experience working with databases, or who are just interested in an introduction to INGRES tools. It focuses on the data handling that can be accomplished using the menu options without exercising any programming knowledge.

The next section of the book, Parts Three and Four, addresses both the original QUEL programming language provided by INGRES and the ANSI standard of SQL programming language. Those installations that have been using INGRES for some time can continue to utilize QUEL, or transition to SQL. In addition to the sections treating each language independently, Appendix E compares the syntax of both languages for easy cross reference.

The final section of the book, Part Five, deals with application programming. A sample application is used to show how the full power of INGRES can be tapped by using INGRES application development tools and INGRES fourth-generation language (4GL).

INGRES is available on many host systems, including a personal computer version. The examples for this book were created on a Digital VAX computer. The book's language is kept as generic as possible, but there will be differences in what certain keys may do on different systems. The local database administrator should be contacted to find out exactly what system and terminal combinations are present.

The book also assumes that the user is an authorized INGRES user and has the authority to create databases. Again, the local DBA should be contacted for access criteria and permission.

■■■ ACKNOWLEDGMENTS

We would like to acknowledge the contributions of the following reviewers: Dr. H. E. Dunsmore, Purdue University; Samuel Hsieh, Vanderbilt University; Kar Yan Tam, University of Texas; and Elizabeth A. Unger, Kansas State University.

We would like to express a special acknowledgment to our families, who have worked with us, and special thanks to Shahrokh Shahmohamadi and Chauncey Williams, who gave us many hours of testing and help. Also to J. Miquelon, for keeping the family together.

Margaret A. Zinky
James W. Everett
Linda J. Hawbaker

CONTENTS

Part 1

INTRODUCTION

Chapter 1

THEORY

INGRES, a product of Ingres Corporation, is an acronym that stands for Interactive Graphics and Retrieval System. INGRES is a relational database management system (DBMS) that can run under various operating systems such as MS-DOS for IBM PCs and compatibles, VMS for the VAX, or UNIX.

The database is manipulated, changed, and viewed by using a database management system in conjunction with a user interface such as one of the query languages, Querying-By-Forms (QBF), or Applications-By-Forms (ABF). The user requests are communicated to the DBMS through one of the various methods that INGRES supports, and the database is acted upon accordingly.

This book is designed so that you can follow the examples and compare figures to the screen on your own terminal. Although there are versions of INGRES expressly tailored for use on personal computers using the other operating systems, our examples were run on a Digital VAX VMS using INGRES version 6.2.

When used on a mainframe level, INGRES can be tailored to operate with many types of terminals. The keyboards on various terminals may be defined to INGRES differently, and are explained in the INGRES manuals. Figure 1.1 on page 4 illustrates how to retrieve information. If you are having problems identifying which keys to use on your terminal, consult the INGRES manuals or contact your system administrator.

■■■ RELATIONAL DATABASES

In a relational database, information is stored in tables. A table is data arranged in a manner that is easy to understand. Tables consist of rows and columns. A row is a record and is read horizontally. A column is a field and is read vertically.

Figure 1.2 shows the cross reference of terms used with a traditional file management system and a relational database.

Tables in a relational database should be constructed to contain logical groupings of information. Suppose you were responsible for maintaining inventory along with the salespeople that sell those parts and the offices where they work. The inventory

```
INGRES/MENU                                    Database: <database_name>

    To run a highlighted command, place the cursor over it and
    select the "GO" menu item.

    Commands    Description

    QUERY       RUN simple or saved QUERY to retrieve, modify or append data
    REPORT      RUN default or saved REPORT

    QBF         Use QUERY-BY-FORMS to develop and test query definitions
    RBF         Use REPORT-BY-FORMS to design or modify reports
    ABF         Use APPLICATIONS-BY-FORMS to design and test applications

    TABLES      CREATE, MANIPULATE or LOOKUP tables in the database
    VIFRED      EDIT forms by using the VISUAL-FORMS-EDITOR
    QUEL        ENTER interactive QUEL statements
    SQL         ENTER interactive SQL statements
    SREPORT     SAVE REPORT-WRITER commands in the reports catalog

Go(Enter)  History()  CommandMode()  DBswitch()  Shell()  >
```

FIGURE 1.1 *RTINGRES Menu*

table	file
row	record
column	field

FIGURE 1.2 *Traditional File Management and Relational Database*

information could easily be obtained by combining data from the inventory table and the salespeople table.

MULTIPLE ROW PROCESSING

One of the primary characteristics of a relational database is that it supports multiple row processing. This means that more than one row can be retrieved, updated, or inserted with only one data manipulation statement. Consider Figure 1.2 and the following statement with Figure 1.3. This single statement would update three rows in the table. This differs from a traditional file management system that only processes one record at a time.

> **update sample**
> **set salesofc = 'Tucson'**
> **where salesofc = 'Phoenix';**

As mentioned before, a relational database stores data in tables. This stored data includes the system database itself, as well as any databases created by end users. Before you decide to store information in a database, the information you want to keep needs to be logically grouped together to assure easy and accurate retrieval and data maintenance.

Imagine that we need to keep track of students and their courses. Consider the relationship of a student and the courses in which she is enrolled. There is a *one to many* relationship between a student and her courses. The table might look something like Figure 1.4.

First we need to determine what will uniquely identify each row in the table. In this case, the student's id will be unique to each student and becomes the *primary key*

lname	salesno	salesofc
Johnson	1001	Phoenix
Castro	1002	Phoenix
Barton	1003	Phoenix
Smith	2001	Las Vegas
Santos	3001	San Diego
Travis	4001	Travis

FIGURE 1.3 *Updated Sales Table*

Name	Id	Course
Smith, Robert Foss, Jill Wright, William	123456789 222334444 999999999	ENG101, MAT105 PSY201, ENG201 ENG201, BPC226

FIGURE 1.4 *Student and Course Table*

for the student and course table. When logically grouping data, generally the following three conditions are undesirable.

- repeating fields (array type data)
- redundant data
- non-dependent data

REPEATING FIELDS

In order to easily manage information, logically group data so that "array" type columns are not used. To remove repeating fields, each student and course enrollment is an individual row in the table. Figure 1.5 shows the result.

REDUNDANT DATA

Notice in the previous example that a student's name may appear multiple times depending on the number of courses in which the student is enrolled. By taking the students' name out of the table and putting it in its own table, we have removed redundant data.

Now, and very importantly, if a student's name changes, only one location will need to be updated as in Figure 1.6.

NON-DEPENDENT DATA

Additionally, we have need to keep track of a student's advisor. The student advisement table in Figure 1.7 shows the advisor assigned to each student. Notice that the department is only dependent on the department number and not on the student's id or the student's advisor.

We need to move data that is non-dependent on the primary key into another table. The table is now composed of two tables as shown in Figure 1.8.

Name	Id	Course
Smith, Robert	123456789	ENG101
Smith, Robert	123456789	MAT105
Foss, Jill	222334444	PSY201
Foss, Jill	222334444	ENG201
Wright, William	999999999	ENG201
Wright, William	999999999	BPC226

FIGURE 1.5 *Student and Course Table*

Name	Id
Smith, Robert	123456789
Foss, Jill	222334444
Wright, William	999999999

Id	Course
123456789	ENG101
123456789	MAT105
222334444	PSY201
222334444	ENG201
999999999	ENG201
999999999	BPC226

FIGURE 1.6 *Student Table (top) and Course Table (bottom)*

Id	Advisor	Department #	Department Title
123456789	Green, Joe	E1000	English
222334444	Hansen, Lou	M2000	Mathematics
999999999	Wilson, Bob	B6000	Business

FIGURE 1.7 *Student Advisement Table*

Id	Advisor	Department #
123456789	Green, Joe	E1000
222334444	Hansen, Lou	M2000
999999999	Wilson, Bob	B6000

Department #	Department Title
E1000	English
M2000	Mathematics
B6000	Business

FIGURE 1.8 *Student Advisement Table (top) and Department Table (bottom)*

These are very general tips for logically grouping data into tables and are not meant to be a comprehensive discussion of database design. Database design is a complete science of its own.

Part 2

INGRES
MENU
SYSTEM

Chapter 2

CREATING TABLES, ENTERING DATA, AND CREATING REPORTS

■ THE INGRES MAIN MENU

Once the database has been created, INGRES can be called by the command, **RTINGRES** <database_name>. The main menu screen shown in Figure 2.1 will appear.

ALTERNATE MAIN MENU SYSTEM

An alternate main menu is available and may be preferred in some installations. Although the menu looks different, the functions it calls are the same. The alternate menu is used by entering the program with the command, **INGMENU** <database_name>. The menu shown in Figure 2.2 will appear.

This menu presents the same functions listed in the RTINGRES main menu. The command choices below the menu allow you to access the various components of the program. Instead of **Shell**, the command to temporarily return to the operating system, some installations may use the command, **Spawn**.

The only significant difference is in the listing for Queries. On the other menu, QBF, SQL, and QUEL had separate listings. On this menu, selecting Queries takes you to the submenu shown in Figure 2.3. From this submenu you select which of the three query systems you wish to use. Once you leave the menus, the screens and commands are identical.

■ CREATING TABLES

Before information can be entered into the newly created database, tables to receive the data must be created. Unlike personal computer database programs, structure in INGRES is not determined when the database is created. Rather, structure is

```
INGRES/MENU                                    Database: <database_name>

   To run a highlighted command, place the cursor over it and
   select the "Go" menu item.

   Commands   Description

   QUERY      RUN simple or saved QUERY to retrieve, modify or append data
   REPORT     RUN default or saved REPORT

   QBF        Use QUERY-BY-FORMS to develop and test query definitions
   RBF        Use REPORT-BY-FORMS to design or modify reports
   ABF        Use APPLICATIONS-BY-FORMS to design and test applications

   TABLES     CREATE, MANIPULATE or LOOKUP tables in the database
   VIFRED     EDIT forms by using the VISUAL-FORMS-EDITOR
   QUEL       ENTER interactive QUEL statements
   SQL        ENTER interactive SQL statements
   SREPORT    SAVE REPORT-WRITER commands in the reports catalog


Go(Enter)  History()  CommandMode()  DBswitch()  Shell()  >
```

FIGURE 2.1   *RTINGRES Menu*

```
Database: <database_name>

                          INGRES/MENU

        ┌────────────────┬─────────────────────────────────────────────┐
        │ Tables         │ Create/examine tables or query/report on table data │
        │ Forms          │ Create/edit/use forms for customized data access │
        │ JoinDefs       │ Create/edit/use join definitions on multiple tables │
        │ Reports        │ Create/edit/run reports                     │
        │ Applications   │ Create/edit/run 4GL applications            │
        │ Queries        │ Query data using Query-By-Forms or a query language │
        │                │                                             │
        └────────────────┴─────────────────────────────────────────────┘

      Place the cursor on your choice and select "Go"


 Go(Enter)   Tables()    Forms()    JoinDefs()    Reports()    >
```

FIGURE 2.2 *INGMENU Menu*

determined for each table as it is created. This gives a tremendous degree of flexibility to the database in INGRES, since no fundamental structure needs to be realigned every time there is a need to add a new type of data to the database. Instead, all that has to be done is to create a new table to hold the new type of data.

NOTE: The table represents the way the user perceives the stored data; it is not the way the data is physically stored in the database. The user does not have to be concerned with the physical storage scheme.

To create the first table for the example database, move the highlight cursor over the TABLES command on the main menu and press **Enter. CAUTION: INGRES distinguishes between the Return key and the Enter key on the VAX numeric keypad.**

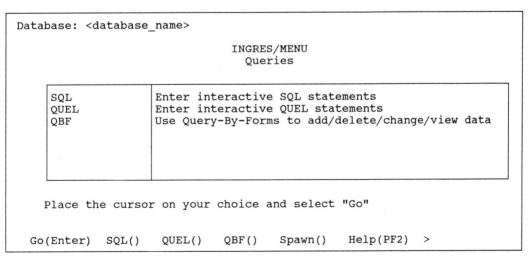

```
Database: <database_name>

                          INGRES/MENU
                            Queries

        ┌────────────────┬─────────────────────────────────────────────┐
        │ SQL            │ Enter interactive SQL statements            │
        │ QUEL           │ Enter interactive QUEL statements           │
        │ QBF            │ Use Query-By-Forms to add/delete/change/view data │
        │                │                                             │
        │                │                                             │
        │                │                                             │
        └────────────────┴─────────────────────────────────────────────┘

      Place the cursor on your choice and select "Go"


 Go(Enter)   SQL()    QUEL()    QBF()    Spawn()    Help(PF2)    >
```

FIGURE 2.3 *Queries Menu*

```
TABLES - Tables Catalog

          ┌──────────────────────────────────────┬──────────┬────────┐
          │ Name                                 │ Owner    │ Type   │
          │                                      │          │        │
          │                                      │          │        │
          │                                      │          │        │
          │                                      │          │        │
          │                                      │          │        │
          │                                      │          │        │
          │                                      │          │        │
          │                                      │          │        │
          │                                      │          │        │
          └──────────────────────────────────────┴──────────┴────────┘

   Place cursor on row and select desired operation from menu.


Create()   Destroy()   Examine()   Query()   Report()   >
```

FIGURE 2.4 *Tables Menu*

They are not interchangeable! The Tables Catalog screen shown in Figure 2.4 will appear. Since this is a new database, the tables catalog is currently empty.

The Tables Catalog screen has its own command menu at the bottom of the screen. Notice that the menu ends in a greater than (>) symbol. This indicates that there are more menu choices available. Pressing the Menu key (PF1) will take the cursor to the menu line, and pressing it again will reveal the remaining choices as indicated below:

   <Report( ) Find( ) Top( ) Bottom( ) Help( ) Quit( ):

The following are the characteristics of the various menu choices:

Create	Creates a new table in the database.
Destroy	Destroys the table that is highlighted by the cursor. You will be asked if you are sure before the table will be deleted.
Examine	Shows the storage information about the table, including structure.
Query	Runs QBF on the table. Allows you to query and update data in the table.
Report	Runs the Report Writer on the table.

Find	Prompts for a string and then searches for it.
Top	Moves the cursor to the top of the list of tables.
Bottom	Moves the cursor to the bottom of the list of tables.
Help	Accesses the help facility.
Quit	Returns to the main menu screen.

To create the first table select **Create**, and the Create a Table screen shown in Figure 2.5 will appear.

The menu choices are described below. **NOTE: Common menu choices that have been previously discussed will not be repeated in the explanatory text.**

Insert	Inserts a new row immediately above the position of the cursor.
Delete	Deletes the row where the cursor is located.
Blank	Clears the entire form of all column data.
Move	Moves the row to where the cursor is located. A submenu will appear with the following choices: Place, Help, End. Move the cursor to the desired location and select **Place**. The row will be inserted before the cursor.
GetTableDef	Prompts for the name of another table and retrieves the specifications. You may call up more than one definition and use the data to create a new combined table using selected fields from the retrieved tables.
Save	Adds the new table to the database.

The cursor is resting on the "Enter the name of the new table" field. When naming a table, you should select a name that will help you to remember what data is in the table. For this example, type in the name **SALESPEOPLE. NOTE: Table names may be up to 36 alphanumeric characters long, and must start with a letter. Column names may also include the underscore.** If a table name is already in use, you will receive an error message and will have to select an alternate name.

After entering the name, press the **Tab** key to advance to the body of the table. Here you will describe the name of the first column. Type **Lname** for last name.

CAUTION: Careful planning is in order here! Unlike dBase III + , INGRES does not have a friendly modify-structure command if you forget to include a needed field. Adding the field later is a cumbersome operation involving the creation of temporary tables and swapping data back and forth. Field length is very important. You must have adequate storage for long names but not waste disk storage space. Taking your time to think exactly what fields you will need in the new table will save a lot of work later!

```
TABLES - Create a Table

Enter the name of the new table:

Enter the column specifications for the new table:

Column Name          Data Type          Key # Nulls Defaults



Insert()   Delete()   Blank()   Move()   GetTableDef()   > :
```

FIGURE 2.5 *Create a Table Menu*

After entering the column name, press the **Tab** key to move to the Data Type column. Available data types are described below:

char(1)–char(2000) String of 1 to 2000 characters.

varchar(1)–varchar (2000) String of 1 to 2000 text characters.

integer1 1-byte integer: $-127 < num < +127$.

smallint 2-byte integer: $-32,767 < num > +32,767$.

integer 4-byte integer: $-2,147,483,647 < num > +2,147,483,647$.

float4 4-byte floating point. Single precision (seven decimals).

float 8-byte floating point. Double precision (16 decimals).

date Date data type (12 bytes).

money Money data type (8 bytes).

The above definitions are based on SQL being the default language at your installation. If QUEL has been made the default language, check the INGRES Menu User's Guide for slight differences in nomenclature for the data format types. For this example, select **char(25)** for the data type of last name.

After entering the appropriate data type and field length, press **Tab** to move to the Key column. Setting up keys allows us to more efficiently use our data later. We will not use Lname as a key field, so tab past the Key column until the highlight is on the Nulls column. Nulls tells the database whether or not to place a null value in the field. This is a special null character that INGRES uses. Nulls are used as defaults only when aggregate functions will be used on the column and an aggregate result will be incorrect without null default. For example, to average all employee ages INGRES would only calculate those columns when age was (not) null. If you chose null, tab past the entry.

Without Null	*With Null*
Age	Age
30	30
40	40
50	50
0	Null
Result: $120/4 = 30$	Result: $120/3 = 40$

If Yes is selected, the Defaults column tells the database to place zeros or blanks in the field if no data is entered. If it is left at the No setting, the database will not leave the field until some data is entered. In effect, it makes the field a required field. Set the default setting at Yes. Press **Return** to move to the next row to enter the next column name.

To complete the table, enter the names and data types listed below. Notice that when we tell the database that Salesno is going to be a key field, the Nulls and Default columns automatically shift to No. In other words, if this is going to be a key field, it must have valid Salesno information in the database.

Column Name	Data Type	Key	Nulls	Defaults
Fname	char(15)		Yes	
Salesno	smallint	1	Yes	
Salesofc	char(25)		Yes	

Once all the data is entered, select **Save** from the Create Table command menu to save the table structure. Since we have elected to use a key for this table, a window appears after Save has been selected to ask whether the key is to be unique or not unique. (See Figure 2.6 on page 19.) When a unique key is selected, it tells the database that there can be no duplicate entries in the key. In other words, no two salespeople can have the same number. It is recommended that unique keys be used. Respond to the prompt by typing "Y."

The first table for the new database is created, but no data has been entered yet. You are once again at the blank Create a Table screen. Before entering data, the other tables that will be used for this part of the book must be created. Using the steps learned above, create the following tables:

CUSTOMER

Cusname	char(25)
Cusaddress	char(25)
Cuscity	char(25)
Cusstate	char(25)
Cuszip	char(25)
Cusphone	char(12)
Cusno	smallint key 1

TRANSACTIONS

Salesno	smallint
Date	date
Cusno	smallint
Partno	smallint
Deldate	date
Qty	smallint
Orderprice	money

INVENTORY

Partno	smallint key 1
Qty	smallint
Itemname	char(30)
Reorder	smallint
Cost	money
Price	money

```
TABLES - Create a Table

Should table have unique keys?

 ┌───────────┬──────────────────────────────────────────┐
 │Unique     │Create table as btree with Unique Keys    │
 │Not Unique │Create table as btree with Non-unique Keys│
 └───────────┴──────────────────────────────────────────┘

   Place the cursor on your choice and select "Go"
```

		#	Nulls	Defaults
fname	char(15)		yes	n/a
salesno	smallint	2	yes	n/a
salesofc	char(25)	3	no	no
			no	no

```
Go(Enter)  Forget(PF3)  Help(PF2)
```

FIGURE 2.6 *Unique Keys Menu*

```
TABLES - Tables Catalog

         ┌──────────────────────────────────┬──────────┬────────┐
         │ Name                             │ Owner    │ Type   │
         ├──────────────────────────────────┼──────────┼────────┤
         │ customer                         │ Username │ table  │
         │ inventory                        │ Username │ table  │
         │ salespeople                      │ Username │ table  │
         │ transactions                     │ Username │ table  │
         │                                  │          │        │
         │                                  │          │        │
         │                                  │          │        │
         │                                  │          │        │
         │                                  │          │        │
         │                                  │          │        │
         │                                  │          │        │
         └──────────────────────────────────┴──────────┴────────┘

    Place cursor on row and select desired operation from menu.

  Create()   Destroy()   Examine()   Query()   Report()    >
```

FIGURE 2.7   *Tables Catalog Screen*

Now that the tables for the database have been created, your Tables Catalog screen should look the same as Figure 2.7 above.

EXAMINING A TABLE

At this time it might be helpful to look at the **Examine** command on the Tables Catalog command menu. With the cursor on any one of the tables that were just created, select the **Examine** command. The screen in Figure 2.8 will appear.

The structure table is self-explanatory, but a few of the terms may need some elaboration.

Owner	Merely reflects the user who created the table.
Row Width	The width in bytes of any row in the table.
Columns	The number of columns or fields in the table.
Rows	The number of rows (data records) in the table. (It is 0 now since we have not entered data.)
Table Type	Shows whether it is a user table, a view, etc.
Storage Structure	Btree unique. Shows that the table has a unique key field.

```
TABLES - Examine a Table

        Information on Table customer

  Owner: Username                Table Type: user table
Row Width: 102            Storage Structure: btree unique
   Columns: 7                  Pages/Overflow: 4/0
      Rows: 0                     Journaling: disabled
```

Column Name	Data Type	Key #	Nulls	Defaults
cusname	char(25)		yes	n/a
cusaddress	char(25)		yes	n/a
cuscity	char(25)		yes	n/a
cusstate	char(2)		yes	n/a
cuszip	char(5)		yes	n/a
cusphone	char(12)		yes	n/a
cusno	i2	1	no	no

```
NewTable()   Find(^F)   Top(^K)   Bottom(^J)   Help(PF2)   End(PF3)
```

FIGURE 2.8 *Examine a Table Screen*

Pages/Overflow	Number of pages occupied by table.
Journaling	Not a user-controlled option. See reference manual.

◼◼ ENTERING AND MANIPULATING DATA

Now that the four tables that are to be used for the examples in this part of the book have been created, it is time to enter data. From the INGRES main menu screen, select **Query** by highlighting the entry and pressing **Return**. The Query Information screen shown in Figure 2.9 appears, asking for the name of the table you wish to query.

Enter the table name **salespeople**, and then select **Go**. The next screen has only a title and a menu at the bottom. Menu choices for this screen are as follows:

Append	Calls the blank default data entry form, and allows data entry.
Retrieve	Allows browsing through the different rows or records in the table.
Update	Allows changing individual items in a row.
Quit	Returns user to the main menu.

Select **Append**, and the blank table screen shown in Figure 2.10 appears.

```
INGRES/MENU
Database: <database_name>


                     QUERY Information


          Enter table name, qbfname, or joindef name:








               Select the "Go" menu item to start QUERY.


   Go(Enter)   Help(PF2)   End(PF3)
```

FIGURE 2.9 *Query Information Screen*

```
                        SALESPEOPLE Table


        Lname:                              Fname:
        Salesno:                            Salesofc:









     Go(Enter)   Blank()    LastQuery()   Order()   Help(PF2)   >
```

FIGURE 2.10 *SALESPEOPLE Blank Record Form*

Enter the data for records in this table from the list of salespeople below. To move from field to field press the **Tab** key. Press **Append** to go to the next blank screen after completing the fields for one salesperson.

Lname	Fname	Salesno	Salesofc
Johnson	Henry	1001	Phoenix
Castro	Robert	1002	Phoenix
Barton	Jane	1003	Phoenix
Smith	John	2001	Las Vegas
Santos	Clarissa	3001	San Diego
Travis	Randy	4001	El Paso

When the data for all the salespeople has been entered, press **End** to end the append operation.

BROWSING THROUGH THE RECORDS

To browse through the records and check the accuracy of your data entry, select **Retrieve**. The following submenu appears at the bottom of the screen:

Go   Runs a selected query.

Blank   Clears all fields so a new query can be run.

Lastquery   Redisplays the values and query operators from the last query.

Order   Sets the sorting order for retrieving data.

Select **Go**, and the first record entered appears. It should be identical to Figure 2.11.

```
                      SALESPEOPLE Table

      Lname: Johnson                          Fname: Henry
      Salesno: 1001                           Salesofc: Phoenix




      Next(Enter)   Query()   Help(PF2)   End(PF3)
```

FIGURE 2.11 *Data for SALESPEOPLE Table*

After cycling through the records to insure that the data is accurate, return to the Query screen with **End**.

CHANGING DATA

The Update function will now be used to correct Johnson's first name. It should be Harry.

Select **Update** from the menu at the bottom of the screen, and then press **Go** to start. The record for Johnson will appear. Use the **Tab** key to move to the Fname field and change the first name to Harry. Press the appropriate key to save the change. A message will appear indicating that the changes are being saved, and the screen will return to a blank record. Press **Quit** to return to the main menu screen.

Now the data for the remaining tables will be entered. Again, select **Query** from the main menu, enter the name of the table, and then select **Append**. Enter the following data for the TRANSACTIONS table:

			TRANSACTIONS Table			
Salesno	*Cusno*	*Partno*	*Date*	*Deldate*	*Qty*	*Price*
1001	8111	9111	20-Feb-89	15-Mar-89	5	9.75
1001	8113	9114	18-Feb-89	28-Feb-89	1	36.99
1002	8113	9113	30-Jul-89	15-Aug-89	10	13.00
1003	8112	9112	15-Jul-89	15-Jul-89	36	5.10
2001	8114	9115	06-Jun-89	30-Jun-89	5	10.90
3001	8116	9111	10-May-89	15-May-89	15	29.25
4001	8115	9114	01-Sep-89	15-Sep-89	2	73.98

Once this table is complete, select **End** and then **Quit** to return to the main menu. Select **Query** again, and enter the data below for the INVENTORY table:

INVENTORY Table					
Partno	*Qty*	*Itemname*	*Reorder*	*Cost*	*Price*
9111	2000	wrench	100	1.35	1.95
9112	100	socket set	20	14.95	21.70
9113	250	scrwdrvr, # 2	50	.89	1.30
9114	60	test meter, M5	10	25.50	36.99
9115	3500	pliers, 3 inch	200	1.50	2.18

Return to the main menu and then select **Query** to enter data into the CUS-TOMER table as indicated below:

CUSTOMER Table						
Cusname	*Cusaddress*	*Cuscity*	*Cusst*	*Cuszip*	*Cusphone*	*Cusno*
Arizona Supply	65 S. Central	Phoenix	Az	85012	602-271-4955	8113
Atlas Supply	1234 W. Thomas	Phoenix	Az	85019	602-235-4311	8111
Desert Vendors	33 N. Outerloop	Las Vegas	Nv	71345	215-333-4111	8114
Ocean Supply	65 Marine Way	San Diego	Ca	24035	591-695-2211	8116
Saguaro Wholesale	351 Highland	Phoenix	Az	85001	602-344-6000	8112
Western Wholesale	2501 Lee Trevino	El Paso	Tx	64311	415-222-6111	8115

■ CREATING REPORTS

To retrieve a report for the SALESPEOPLE table, select the **Report** option on the main menu. The Report Information screen shown in Figure 2.12 appears.

Since no special report files have been created yet, we will use the default report formats to look at the data in the SALESPEOPLE table. Feel free to experiment with the following steps as no damage can be done at this point. After typing in the name of the table press **Tab** to advance to the next item on the Report Information screen, which offers the following three choices:

report   If a report and a table have the same name, run the report.

table   If a report and a table have the same name, run the table.

any   This is the default setting that tells the system to run a predefined report (either a special format or the default).

```
INGRES/MENU
Database: <database_name>


                     REPORT Information


   Enter a table name or a report name:


   Change default options if desired:

       Type ("report", "table", "any"): any

       Suppress REPORT status messages ("y", "n")? n

       For a report on table above, enter report style
       ("block", "column", "wrap" or "default"): default

       Output File Name:
       (Report goes to terminal if blank)


   Select the "Go" menu item to start REPORT.



   Go(Enter)  Help(PF2)  End(PF3)
```

FIGURE 2.12 *Report Information Screen*

The next item, "Suppress REPORT status messages," will stop the message display at the bottom of the screen. This is normally left at "n." The next item, "report style," has the following choices:

block	Each record is shown as a single block. See Figure 2.13. The block format may not fit on an 80-column printer, and the compressed mode may be required.
column	Each record is presented in a row. See Figure 2.14.
wrap	Same style as column, but it automatically wraps the record to the next line as required by the output specifications. Column style may or may not wrap depending upon the output device.
default	Tells INGRES to decide which is the best style for the particular table or report.

The next item asks for an output file name. In the absence of a file name the report will be displayed on the screen. When you want a printout of the report, enter a file name here. Although a suffix is not required, it is a good idea to add a suffix, such as .rpt, to readily identify report files in your directory. If you have assigned a

```
 15-FEB-1989                                        07:31:10

                   Report on Table: salespeople
                   ------ -- ----- -----------

     Lname: Barton          Fname: Jane          Salesno:       1003
     Salesofc: Phoenix

     Lname: Castro          Fname: Robert        Salesno:       1002
     Salesofc: Phoenix

     Lname: Johnson         Fname: Harry         Salesno:       1001
     Salesofc: Phoenix

     Lname: Santos          Fname: Clarissa      Salesno:       3001
     Salesofc: San Diego

     Lname: Smith           Fname: John          Salesno:       2001
     Salesofc: Las Vegas

     Lname: Travis          Fname: Randy         Salesno:       4001
     Salesofc: El Paso
```

FIGURE 2.13 *SALESPEOPLE Report, Block Option*

name to the report and then press **Enter**, the report will be placed in the file in your directory, but it will not be immediately printed out. It will not appear on the screen either; instead, a screen will appear indicating that the report is being set up and that the data is being retrieved and sorted. After this message, the screen will return to the main menu.

PRINTING A REPORT

At the main menu screen select **Shell**, which will return you to the system command prompt. Here issue the system command to send the report file to the system printer. After the acknowledgement message, type the log-off command for your system to return to the INGRES main menu. You may need assistance for printing and logging

```
 15-FEB-1989                                        07:31:10

                   Report on Table: SALESPEOPLE
                   ------ -- ----- -----------

     Lname          Fname        Salesno   Salesofc
     -----          -----        -------   --------
     Barton         Jane         1003      Phoenix
     Castro         Robert       1002      Phoenix
     Johnson        Harry        1001      Phoenix
     Santos         Clarissa     3001      San Diego
     Smith          John         2001      Las Vegas
     Travis         Randy        4001      El Paso
```

FIGURE 2.14 *SALESPEOPLE Report, Column Option*

off, but generally typing **print** < file name > will print to the default printer, then you can log off.

Creating reports for the remaining tables will result in the printouts shown in Figures 2.15 through 2.17. With the tables created, the menu system will allow you to append, update, or delete any data in the tables. You may also print out reports on the tables either on the screen or on the system printer. So far, however, only the default options have been used. The next chapter discusses creating or modifying input/output forms and creating customized reports.

```
21-aug-1990                                                        22:26:41

                            Report on Table: transactions

Salesno   Cusno   Partno   Date          Deldate       Qty   Orderprice
-------   -----   ------   -----------   -----------   ---   ----------
1001      8111    9111     20-feb-1989   15-mar-1989    5    $  9.75
          8113    9114     18-feb-1989   28-feb-1989    1    $ 36.99
1002      8113    9113     30-jan-1989   28-feb-1989   10    $ 13.00
1003      8112    9112     15-feb-1989   01-mar-1989    3    $ 65.10
2001      8114    9115     31-jan-1989   28-feb-1989    5    $ 10.90
3001      8116    9111     10-feb-1989   15-mar-1989   15    $ 29.25
4001      8115    9114     05-feb-1989   28-feb-1989    2    $ 73.98
```

FIGURE 2.15 *Transactions Table*

```
20-aug-1990                                                22:13:38

                           Report on Table: inventory

Partno   Qty   Description                Reorder    Cost      Price
------   ----  -----------                -------    ----      -----
9111     2000  Wrench                         100   $ 1.35    $ 1.95
9112      100  Socket set                      20   $14.95    $21.70
9113      250  Screwdriver, phillips #2        50   $  .89    $ 1.30
9114       60  Test meter, M5                  10   $25.50    $36.99
9115     3500  Pliers, 3 inch                 200   $ 1.50    $ 2.18
```

FIGURE 2.16 *Inventory Table*

```
20-aug-1990                                                                            22:13:16

                                      Report on Table: customer
                                      ------ -- -------  --------

Cusname            Cusaddress       Cuscity     Cusstate   Cuszip   Cusphone        Cusno
-------            ----------       -------     --------   ------   --------        -----
Arizona Supply     65 S. Central    Phoenix     Az         85012    602-271-4955    8113
Atlas Supply       1234 W. Thomas   Phoenix     Az         85019    602-235-4311    8111
Desert Vendors     33. N. Outerloop Las Vegas   Nv         71345    215-333-4111    8114
Ocean Supply       65 Marine Way    San Diego   Ca         24035    591-695-2211    8116
Saguaro Wholesale  351 Highland     Phoenix     Az         85001    602-344-6000    8112
Western Wholesale  2501 Lee Trevino El Paso     Tx         64311    415-222-6111    8115
```

FIGURE 2.17 *Customer Table*

Chapter 3

CUSTOMIZING FORMS AND REPORTS

To create customized data entry forms select **VIFRED** on the main menu screen. This will bring up the Visual-Forms-Editor information screen shown in Figure 3.1.

For this example we will use the TRANSACTIONS table to create a form that a data entry clerk might use when taking a phone order. Since there is no form yet, enter the name **transactions**. Press **Tab** to go to the next item, change "form" to **table**, and then select **Go**. The screen shown in Figure 3.2 will appear showing the default layout for the fields in the TRANSACTIONS table. This is a good starting point for developing a custom form, since all of the data fields are shown on the screen.

```
INGRES/MENU                                    Database: <database_name>
                    VISUAL-FORMS-EDITOR Information
         Enter form name, table name or joindef name:


         Change default options if desired:

             Type ("form", "table", "joindef"): form






             Select the "Go" menu item to start VISUAL-FORMS-EDITOR.


    Go(Enter)  Help(PF2)   End(PF3)
```

FIGURE 3.1 *VISUAL-FORMS-EDITOR Information Screen*

```
                         TRANSACTIONS Table

        Salesno: f_____                      Cusno: f_____
         Partno: f_____                       Date: c_____
        Deldate: c_____     Qty: f_____
      Orderprice: $_____.__




      ------------------------------End-of-Form------------------------------------



      Create()    Delete()    Edit()    Move()    Undo(.)   Order()    >
```

FIGURE 3.2 *TRANSACTIONS Table Form*

Notice that each field is displayed with the name of the field, the type of data to be entered into the field, and a line representing the length of the field. The end-of-form line will automatically adjust as we rearrange the fields on the form. The menu choices along the bottom of the screen are discussed below:

Create	Creates a new component at the current cursor position. A submenu offers choices of the type of component.
Delete	Deletes the component or blank line the cursor is on.
Edit	Edits the selected component. A submenu offers choices.
Move	Prepares to move the selected component to a new location. A submenu gives movement options.
Undo	Cancels the last command that changed the form. You can also undo an undo.
Order	Changes the sequence of fields within the form.
Formattributes	Allows selection of full screen (default) size for the new form, or pop-up size.
Location	Returns the current row and column position of the cursor.

ENTERING TITLES AND LETTERHEADS

To start customizing the form, we will put a company letterhead and a new form title at the top of the form. All of the items that are not actual fields in the database are referred to as *trim* in INGRES. Select **Create** from the screen, and the following submenu will appear:

Trim	Creates up to 150 characters of trim at the cursor location. End trim insertion with Menu key.
Field	Creates a new input/output field. A submenu will appear showing components of the field.
TableField	Creates a new table field at cursor location. Puts you in the table field creation screen (see reference manuals for this subject).
NewLine	Creates a blank line *above* the cursor.
Boxline	A line component is a box with only one row or column, a one-dimensional box. Boxes can overlay other boxes, but if overlapped by another component will be obscured.

With the cursor on the top line select **Create** and **NewLine**. A blank line will appear. Do this several more times to make enough space for a letterhead. Put the cursor on the "T" of the current title, "TRANSACTION TABLE" and select **Delete**. This clears the area for our new title. Select **Create** again, and then select **Trim**. Now type the following title:

ARIZONA WIDGET WHOLESALE SUPPLY COMPANY

Press the **Menu** key to mark the end of the trim insertion. With the cursor still on this line select **Move**, and then select **Center**. The main title line is now on the form and centered. Add the next three lines of trim centered just below the main title using the same procedures.

234 N. CENTRAL AVENUE
PHOENIX, ARIZONA 85001
602-251-6000

Leave one blank line under the phone number and insert the form title:

CUSTOMER ORDER FORM

MOVING AND EDITING FIELDS

Now place the cursor over the Cusno field and select **Move**. Move the cursor to the top left of the form, two lines under the heading, and select **Place**. The entire field will move to the new location. **NOTE: Look at the completed form in Figure 3.3 to get a picture of where we are heading with this form.**

Select **Edit**, and then select **Title** to change the field's abbreviated name to

```
+----------------------------------------------------------------------+
|              ARIZONA WIDGET WHOLESALE SUPPLY COMPANY                  |
|                     234 N. CENTRAL AVENUE                             |
|                   PHOENIX, ARIZONA  85001                             |
|                       602-251-6000                                   |
|                                                                      |
|                     CUSTOMER ORDER FORM                              |
|                                                                      |
|  CUSTOMER NUMBER: f_____           SALESPERSON: f_____             |
|                                                                      |
|                 PART NUMBER: f_____                                 |
|                                                                      |
|     QUANTITY ORDERED: f_____          ORDER PRICE: $_____.__   |
|                                                                      |
|  DATE: c_____     REQ DEL DATE: c_____     |
|                                                                      |
|                                                                      |
|  -----------------------------End-of-Form--------------------------- |
|    Create()   Delete()   Edit()   Move()   Undo(.)   Order()   >     |
+----------------------------------------------------------------------+
```

FIGURE 3.3 *Customer Form*

CUSTOMER NUMBER. Do not be alarmed if the field seems to disappear as you type the new title over it; it will reappear when you press the **Menu** key to signify that editing is complete.

CHANGING FIELD ATTRIBUTES

Before we leave this field, we can change the attributes to make the form more usable. Select **Edit** again, and then select **Attributes**. The screen in Figure 3.4 will appear to allow you to modify the various attributes of the field. The box on the left refers to the display attributes on the screen when the form is used, and the text on the right allows for applying validation criteria to data as it is entered.

Display Attributes. Display attributes that are not self-explanatory are explained below:

Box Field	Draws a box around the field.
Keep Previous Value	Copies the value that was entered into field on the previous form.
Mandatory Field	User must enter a value.
Query Only	User can enter value only in query state.
Force Lower Case	Uppercase automatically converted to lowercase. Opposite in Force Upper Case.
No Auto Tab	Reaching end of field does not cause automatic tabbing to next field.
No Echo	Data entered is not visible. Used for password entries.

```
┌─────────────────────────────────────────────────────────────────────┐
│ VIFRED - Attributes for Field                                         │
│                        Data Type: i2              Nullable: n         │
│ ┌──────────────────────────┬─────┐                                    │
│ │ Attribute                │ Set │  Default Value for Field:          │
│ ├──────────────────────────┼─────┤                                    │
│ │ Box Field                │ n   │                                    │
│ │ Keep Previous Value      │ n   │  Internal Name for Field:          │
│ │ Mandatory Field          │ n   │     cusno                          │
│ │ Reverse Video            │ n   │                                    │
│ │ Blinking                 │ n   │  Validation Check to Perform on Field: │
│ │ Underline                │ n   │                                    │
│ │ Brightness Change        │ n   │                                    │
│ │ Query Only               │ n   │                                    │
│ │ Force Lower Case         │ n   │                                    │
│ │ Force Upper Case         │ n   │                                    │
│ │ No Auto Tab              │ n   │                                    │
│ │ No Echo                  │ n   │  Validation Error Message:         │
│ │ Display Only             │ n   │                                    │
│ │ Invisible                │ n   │                                    │
│ │ END OF ATTRIBUTES        │     │  Color: 0                          │
│ └──────────────────────────┴─────┘                                    │
│                                                                       │
│  Help(PF2)   End(PF3)                                                 │
└─────────────────────────────────────────────────────────────────────┘
```

FIGURE 3.4   *VIFRED's Field Attributes Screen .*

Display Only   User cannot type anything into the field.

Invisible   Does not display this field.

Note that Mandatory Field is already selected. This is because we previously designated Cusno as a key field.

Validation Checks.   On the right side of the attribute screen are some of the parameters of the field itself. Of interest now are the two lines pertaining to the validation check. The validation check allows us to control the data entered into the form to help prevent a data entry operator from making errors. We are going to place a simple validation check in the Customer Number field. After the data entry clerk enters the number, INGRES will check the table that contains that field to insure that the number entered is, in fact, a valid number that exists in the database. If not, the error message we select will be printed on the form and the number will not be accepted.

Tab to the area labeled "Validation Check to Perform" and enter the following statement:

cusno in customer.cusno

What we in effect are saying is, "Check for the just entered Cusno in the Customer table and the Cusno column." If there is a match, the program will continue to accept data. If not, then a message will appear. **Tab** to the next area of the form, "Validation Error Message," and type in the following message:

Invalid customer number, check and reenter.

To complete the form as shown in Figure 3.3, repeat the above procedures to move and edit the remaining fields. Press **Menu** key at completion. Select Mandatory Field for all fields on the form except for required delivery date. When you get to the Salesperson and Part Number fields, enter the validation as indicated below:

salesno in salespeople.salesno
partno in inventory.partno

Insert appropriate error messages in the validation error message space for each of these fields.

FIELD ORDER

There is one step left to make the form more efficient to use. We have moved fields around on the form, thus changing their tabbing order. If you tried to enter data now, the cursor would jump from field to field based on the original order of the fields on the form. To see this, select **Order,** and the form will appear as shown in Figure 3.5. The numbers indicate the original tabbing order and show that the cursor would go to Salesperson first. The two menu choices of interest are:

```
        ARIZONA WIDGET WHOLESALE SUPPLY COMPANY
                234 N. CENTRAL AVENUE
                PHOENIX, ARIZONA 85001
                    602-251-6000

                  CUSTOMER ORDER FORM




   CUSTOMER NUMBER: 2                      SALESPERSON: 1

                  PART NUMBER: 3

      QUANTITY ORDERED: 6            ORDER PRICE: 7


 DATE: 4                        REQ DEL DATE: 5




 Edit()    Defaultorder()    Forget(.)    Help()    End()
```

FIGURE 3.5 *Field Order*

Edit	Selecting edit with the cursor on a field allows individual tabbing order to be changed.
Defaultorder	Directs the program to resequence all fields. Default sequence is left to right, top to bottom.

Select **Defaultorder**, and the numbers will change to the normal sequence.

FORM ATTRIBUTES

One menu choice that we have not examined is the Formattributes command, which can be seen by scrolling past the Order command on the menu. When selected, a Form Attributes miniscreen appears as shown in Figure 3.6. This screen allows a choice between having the form cover the entire screen (the default mode), or having the form appear as a pop-up form on top of another form that is in use. Select **End** to leave the form in its default size.

◼ SAVING A FORM

Now that the custom form is complete select **Save,** and the Saving a Form screen shown in Figure 3.7 will appear. Notice that the name of the form is still the name of the table. Change it to **customerorder** to more readily show its use. **Tab** to "Short Remark" and enter a short phrase to show the form's use. Select **Save** again to save the renamed form. Once the form is saved you are returned to the customer order screen. Select **Quit** to return to the main menu.

When we first selected VIFRED no forms existed, so we used a table name to start customizing the table default form. Once forms have been saved, the VIFRED

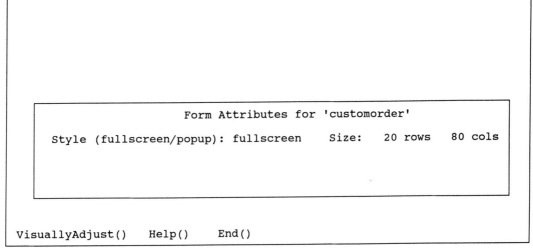

FIGURE 3.6 *Form Attributes Screen*

```
VIFRED - Saving a Form

 Name: transactions                          Created:

Owner: Username                              Modified:

Short Remark:

 Long Remark:
┌──────────────────────────────────────────────────────────────┐
│                                                                │
│                                                                │
│                                                                │
│                                                                │
│                                                                │
│                                                                │
│                                                                │
└──────────────────────────────────────────────────────────────┘


    Save()     Forget()     Help()
```

FIGURE 3.7 *Form Saving*

Forms Catalog shown in Figure 3.8 can be accessed from the VIFRED Information screen by selecting **Go** without typing in any table or form name.

If **Create** is selected from the catalog screen, a submenu appears with the following choices:

```
VIFRED - Forms Catalog

┌────────────────────┬──────────┬──────────────────────────────┐
│ Name               │ Owner    │ Short Remark                 │
├────────────────────┼──────────┼──────────────────────────────┤
│ customerorder      │ Username │ TO ENTER A CUSTOMER ORDER    │
│ newcustomer        │ Username │                              │
│                    │          │                              │
│                    │          │                              │
│                    │          │                              │
│                    │          │                              │
│                    │          │                              │
│                    │          │                              │
└────────────────────┴──────────┴──────────────────────────────┘

       Place cursor on row and select desired operation from menu.

   Create()    Destroy()    Edit()    Rename()    MoreInfo()    >
```

FIGURE 3.8 *Forms Catalog*

Blankform	Starts with a blank screen to design a new form.
Tabledefault	Uses a table's default form as the starting point for the new form.
Joindefreport	Uses a previously defined join definition of two or more tables as the starting point for the new form.

Two other menu choices that are new are **MoreInfo,** which displays the Saving a Form screen information about the current form, and **Utilities,** which presents a sub-menu with the following choices:

Compile	Used by programmers. See SQL or QUEL guides.
Print	Creates a print file in your directory that when printed shows a copy of the form and the specifications about all of the fields and trim used in the form.
QBFnames	Displays a catalog of all QBF names that are associated with the form.

◼ ENTERING DATA INTO A CUSTOM FORM

Now that our form is completed and saved, we will enter a trial transaction using the new customer order form to check our validation selections. Incorrect data will be entered to test the form's capabilities. From the main menu select **QBF** or Query-By-Forms.

When the Query screen appears as shown in Figure 3.9, enter **customerorder.** Select **Go** and then **Append** from the QBF execution screen. The customer order screen appears and the cursor is on the first field, ready to accept data.

Enter **9500** (an invalid number) and press **Tab** to move to the next field. The computer displays an error message at the bottom of the screen and does not leave the first field. Now enter a correct number **(8111).** After the computer checks it against the allowable numbers in the CUSTOMER table, it records the data and moves to the next field.

Enter incorrect numbers for both the salesperson and the part number and observe that the same error message occurs. Enter correct data and **Tab** to the Date field. Attempt to bypass this field by tabbing to Required Delivery Date; again the computer will not allow you to pass up a mandatory field. Enter the date **100389,** and INGRES will change it to its own date format. Do not put a value in Required Delivery Date. This is acceptable since we did not declare this as a mandatory field.

Select **Append,** and the data is added as a record in the TRANSACTIONS table. The screen returns to a blank customer order form ready for the next transaction. Select **End,** and the computer returns to the QBF execution screen after printing a message that the data was added to the table. Select **Quit** to return to the main menu.

To insure that the data was properly added to the table, select **Query** and **Go**

```
INGRES/MENU                                    Database: <database_name>
                        QUERY-BY-FORMS Information


   Enter table name, qbfname, or joindef name:



   Change default options if desired:

         Type ("table", "qbfname", "joindef" or "any"): any

         If a table is specified, indicate if a table field is to be used
            ("y", "n"): n

   Select the "Go" menu item to start QUERY-BY-FORMS.



   Go(Enter)  Help(PF2)  End(PF3)
```

FIGURE 3.9 *QUERY-BY-FORMS Information Screen*

from the main menu. Select **transactions** as the table choice, and then **Retrieve** to look at the data. Press **Go** to start the query, and the first record in the table will appear. Use the **Next** key to cycle through the records, and the last record should contain the data we just entered through our customer form. Select **End** and then **Quit** to return to the main menu.

For additional practice, prepare a New Customer data input form for the customer table so that it matches the form shown in Figure 3.10.

```
                        NEW CUSTOMER ENTRY FORM
                  Arizona Widget Wholesale Supply Company


   Cusname: c_____        Cusno: f_____

      Cusadd: c_____

      Cuscity: c_____

      Cusstate: c_      Cuszip: c_____

     ·Cusphone: c_____
   --------------------------End-of-Form--------------------------------



         Go(Enter)  Blank()  LastQuery()  Order()  Help()  >
```

FIGURE 3.10 *New Customer Entry Form*

CUSTOMIZING REPORTS

Creating customized reports is almost identical to creating customized forms. From the main menu select **RBF** and then **Go**. The Report-By-Forms screen appears as shown in Figure 3.11.

Enter the table name **customer** and select **Go** to start building a customer phone list. The table default screen appears as shown in Figure 3.12, and it looks the same as the initial screen for designing an input form. Not only does it look the same, but the commands we will use are identical to the editing commands for editing forms!

To start, move the cursor over the "R" in the current title, "Report on Table: customer," and select **Delete**. Select **Create** and then **Trim** and enter the title below:

CUSTOMER PHONE LIST

Now select **Move** and **Center** to place the title centered on the line. Put the cursor on the detail line and insert a blank line to hold the column headings. Select **Create** and **Line** to accomplish this. Look at Figure 3.13 to see what the completed report form will look like.

DELETING FIELDS

Enter the column headings as shown in Figure 3.13 by moving the cursor to the desired location and selecting **Create** and **Trim**. Now move the cursor to the field area. We will first delete all of the fields except Cusname, Cusno, and Cusphone. Move to Cusaddress, place the cursor over the field type symbol (c), and select **Delete**. Both

```
INGRES/MENU                                        Database: <database_name>
                           REPORT-BY-FORMS Information



     Enter a table name or a report name:

     Change default options if desired:

         Type ("report", "table", "any"): any

         Suppress RBF status messages ("y", "n")? n

         For report on table above, enter report style
         ("block", "column", "wrap" or "default"): default



     Select the "Go" menu item to start REPORT-BY-FORMS.


 Go(Enter)  Help(PF2)  End(PF3)
```

FIGURE 3.11 *REPORT-BY-FORMS Information Screen*

```
-------------------------------------Title--------------------------------------
                    Report on Table: customer

------------------------------Column-Headings-----------------------------------
-------------------------------Detail-Lines-------------------------------------
Cusname: c_____
Cusaddress: c_____
Cuscity: c_____         Cusstate: c_
Cuszip: c____           Cusphone: c_____      Cusno: f_____

------------------------------End-of-Detail-------------------------------------




    Create()   Delete()   Edit()   Move()   Undo(.)   Order()   >
```

FIGURE 3.12   *Customer Report*

the field name and the field length indicator will disappear. Repeat this process for Cuscity, Cusstate, and Cuszip.

Now place the cursor over the first letter of the field name Cusname and select **Delete**. The field name disappears, but this time the field length indicator remains in place. Now you will move the field length indicator under the appropriate column

```
-------------------------------------Title--------------------------------------
                    CUSTOMER PHONE LIST

------------------------------Column-Headings-----------------------------------
CUSTOMER NAME                         NUMBER                    PHONE
-------------------------------Detail-Lines-------------------------------------
c_____                f_____                    c_____
------------------------------End-of-Detail-------------------------------------






    Create()   Delete()   Edit()   Move()   Undo(.)   Order()   >
```

FIGURE 3.13   *Customer Phone List Form*

heading. Place the cursor over the field type indicator and select **Move**. Move the cursor until it lines up under the column heading CUSTOMER NAME and select **Place**. Repeat these steps to delete the Cusphone and Cusno field names and to align their field length indicators under the appropriate headings. After you delete any blank lines under the new field line the form should be identical to Figure 3.13.

▄▄▄ PRINT OPTIONS

The report is not quite complete, however. There are some options that we can select to control how the report will look when it is printed out. First select **ReportOptions** and the screen in Figure 3.14 will appear.

This screen shows the default page length for both a report sent to a terminal or to a printer, the default underlining character, and whether to insert formfeeds (usually No). In addition it asks what characters are to be used to display null values. The bottom half of the screen allows control of the underlining of titles within the report. Depending on your printer, you may change report length for a written report, but most of these values stay at their default settings.

SORTING THE DATA

Select **Order** at the Report screen to bring up the Order Columns screen shown in Figure 3.15.

This screen allows us to establish the sorting order, whether the sort will be ascending or descending, and where control breaks will occur. Since this is a simple

```
RBF - Report Options

         Page Length (lines):          (Default is 23 when report is written
                                         to a terminal and 61 to a file.)

      Underlining Character:           (Default is '-' when report is written
                                         to a terminal and '_' to a file.)

    Insert Formfeeds (y/n): n

    Display Null Values as:

=====================================================================================

  Specify the underlining to be done in each of the following sections.

     In report title section: 1              The codes to use are:
                                     --------------------------------------------
  In column headings section: 1      ('a' - underline all the text in section)
                                     ('l' - underline the last line only)
         In detail section: n        ('n' - underline none of the text)


  Help(PF2)   End(PF3)
```

FIGURE 3.14 *Report Options Screen*

```
RBF - Order Columns


     Scroll through the column names.  Select the sorting sequence (0 - 127),
     sorting direction ("a" or "d") and whether to break ("y" or "n") for each
     column.
```

Column Name	Sequence	Direction	Break?
cusname	1	a	n
cusadd	0		
cuscity	0		
cusstate	0		
cuszip	0		
cusphone	0		
cusno	0		

```
     ColumnOptions()   Top(^K)   Bottom(^J)   Help(PF2)   End(PF3)
```

FIGURE 3.15   *Order Columns Screen*

phone list, the only item of interest here is to select Cusname to sort by. To do this type a **1** in the Sequence column next to Cusname, type **a** in the Direction column for ascending, and finally **n** in the Break column. We will discuss the remainder of this screen when we create the next report.

■ SAVING A REPORT

Return to the report format and select **Save**. The Saving a Report screen will appear. It is identical to the screen for saving a custom form. Name the report **phonelist** then select **Save** again. Now the Report Catalog screen shown in Figure 3.16 appears.

There are two new menu items on this screen, although they are on the hidden portion of the menu. Pressing the Menu key twice reveals the second line of the menu and the two new choices:

Autoreport	You will be asked for a table name, and then the program will select one of the default report options to create the report.
Utilities	Archive writes the report to a text file in Report Writer language. The file can be edited but can no longer be used in RBF. It must then be reentered through SREPORT. Archive is similar to storage. You can find it, but you cannot recall it for use interactively.

```
RBF - Report Catalog

┌──────────────────────┬──────────┬───────────────────────────┐
│ Name                 │ Owner    │ Short Remark              │
├──────────────────────┼──────────┼───────────────────────────┤
│ phonelist            │ Username │ RBF                       │
│                      │          │                           │
│                      │          │                           │
│                      │          │                           │
│                      │          │                           │
│                      │          │                           │
│                      │          │                           │
└──────────────────────┴──────────┴───────────────────────────┘

          Place cursor on row and select desired operation from menu.

   Create()   Destroy()   Edit()   Rename()   MoreInfo()   >
```

FIGURE 3.16   *RBF Report Catalog Screen*

Select **End** and you will be returned to the main menu. Our report form is complete.

When we want to use the report we select **Report** at the main menu, and the Report Information screen shown in Figure 3.17 will appear. Enter **phonelist** and then select **Go**. The report shown in Figure 3.18 will appear. We will discuss printing a copy of a report in the next report that we build.

```
INGRES/MENU                                    Database: <database_name>
                        REPORT Information

    Enter a table name or a report name:

    Change default options if desired:

        Type ("report", "table", "any"): any

        Suppress REPORT status messages ("y", "n")? n

        For a report on table above, enter report style
        ("block", "column", "wrap" or "default"): default

        Output File Name:
        (Report goes to terminal if blank)

    Select the "Go" menu item to start REPORT.

   Go(Enter)   Help(PF2)   End(PF3)
```

FIGURE 3.17   *REPORT Information Screen*

```
                   CUSTOMER PHONE LIST
                   -------- ----- ----

     CUSTOMER NAME            NUMBER              PHONE
     -------------            ------              -----
     Arizona Supply            8113           602-271-4955
     Atlas Supply              8111           602-235-4311
     Desert Vendors            8114           215-333-4111
     Ocean Supply              8112           602-344-6000
     Western Wholesale         8115           415-222-6111
```

FIGURE 3.18   *Customer Phone List Report*

Next we will create a Sales Activity report using the TRANSACTIONS table. You should be familiar now with the editing commands for creating reports. Create a report format identical to that shown in Figure 3.19.

MULTIPLE SORTS

After you have finished the editing select **Order,** and the Order Columns screen appears. We are going to tell the computer how and in what priority to sort the data in the table to produce the report we just designed. Type **1** in the Sequence column opposite Salesno, and type **2** opposite Cusno. This tells the program that the primary sorting is to be done by Salesno, and that if there is more than one customer for a salesperson the customers should be sorted in order.

Now type **a** in the Direction column for both Salesno and Cusno to tell the program to sort in ascending order. Finally, type **y** in the Break column for Salesno. "Break," or more commonly "control break," tells the computer that each time the Salesno changes to a different salesperson the report should be segmented so that

```
---------------------------------------Title-------------------------------------

                         SALES ACTIVITY REPORT
                  Arizona Widget Wholesale Supply Company

-------------------------------Column-Headings----------------------------------
 Salesman       Customer     Part               Amount            Date
-------------------------------Detailed-Lines-----------------------------------

 f_____        f_____   f_____     $_____.__    c_____
-------------------------------End-of-Form--------------------------------------




 Create()   Delete()   Edit()   Move()   Undo(.)   Order()   >
```

FIGURE 3.19   *Sales Activity Report Format*

each salesperson's data is in a separate portion of the report. When you are finished the screen should look like Figure 3.20.

■■■ COLUMN OPTIONS

Now move the cursor down to the Orderprice field and select **ColumnOptions,** and the Column Options screen will appear as shown in Figure 3.21. Type an **x** in the Over Report and Over Breaks columns opposite the Sum entry. Here we are telling the program to sum the Orderprice field and to display that sum for each salesperson whenever there is a break for a Salesno change in the report. Additionally, a final total for all salespeople will be printed at the end of the report.

Now the report is complete. Select **End** until you return to the report format and then select **Save**. When the Saving a Report screen appears, name the report **salesactivity**.

■■■ PRINTING A REPORT

To print the report, select **Report** and **Go** from the main menu. On the Report Information screen enter **salesactivity**, and then **Tab** down to the Output File Name: field. Enter the report name **sales.rpt** and select **Go**. The report does not immediately print out, but rather you are returned to the main menu screen. Select **Shell** and you are returned to your system prompt. At the system prompt, enter the system command that will cause your report file to be printed. After the print command is acknowledged by the system, type in the normal system log-off command and you will be returned to the main menu. Your report should look like Figure 3.22.

Continue practicing the commands you have learned in this chapter by creating the Inventory Status report shown in Figure 3.23 using the INVENTORY table.

In this section of the book we have discussed handling data using the menu system. Although this gives us a fairly wide range of options, we are still limited to what the simple tables and forms can do. The following sections of the book deal with the built-in programming languages and with developing applications using forms. This opens a whole new range of possibilities for combining data from more than one table, and for embedding commands to eliminate many keystrokes and increase our flexibility in using data to solve problems.

```
- Order Columns

    Scroll through the column names.  Select the sorting sequence (0 - 127),
    sorting direction ("a" or "d") and whether to break ("y" or "n") for each
    column.
    ┌──────────────────────────────────┬──────────┬───────────┬────────┐
    │ Column Name                      │ Sequence │ Direction │ Break? │
    ├──────────────────────────────────┼──────────┼───────────┼────────┤
    │ salesno                          │ 1        │ a         │ y      │
    │ cusno                            │ 2        │ a         │ n      │
    │ partno                           │ 0        │           │        │
    │ date                             │ 0        │           │        │
    │ deldate                          │ 0        │           │        │
    │ qty                              │ 0        │           │        │
    │ orderprice                       │ 0        │           │        │
    │                                  │          │           │        │
    │                                  │          │           │        │
    │                                  │          │           │        │
    └──────────────────────────────────┴──────────┴───────────┴────────┘

   ColumnOptions()   Top(^K)   Bottom(^J)   Help(PF2)   End(PF3)
```

FIGURE 3.20 *Order Column*

```
RBF - Column options

  Column Name:  orderprice                      Break Column:  n


  Selection Criteria at run time:  n     (n = none, v = value, r = range)

        Enter "x" to select Aggregate/Break combinations for columns
      ┌──────────────┬─────────────┬─────────────┬────────────┐
      │ Aggregate    │ Over Report │ Over Breaks │ Over Pages │
      ├──────────────┼─────────────┼─────────────┼────────────┤
      │ Any          │             │             │            │
      │ Average      │             │             │            │
      │ Count        │             │             │            │
      │ Maximum      │             │             │            │
      │ Minimum      │             │             │            │
      │ Sum          │ x           │ x           │            │
      │              │             │             │            │
      └──────────────┴─────────────┴─────────────┴────────────┘


      Help(PF2)   End(PF3)
```

FIGURE 3.21 *Column Options Screen*

```
                          SALES ACTIVITY REPORT
                Arizona Widget Wholesale Supply Company
                ------- ------ ---------- ------ -------

Salesman      Customer     Part             Amount      Date
--------      --------     ----             ------      ----
 1001           8111       9111           $  9.75    20-feb-1989
                8111       9114           $ 36.99    03-oct-1989
                8113       9114           $ 36.99    18-feb-1989
-----------------------------------------------------------------
Totals:  1001
Sum:                                      $ 83.73
-----------------------------------------------------------------

  1002          8113       9113           $ 13.00    30-jul-1989
-----------------------------------------------------------------
Totals:  1002
Sum:                                      $ 13.00
-----------------------------------------------------------------


  1003          8112       9112           $ 65.10    15-jul-1989
-----------------------------------------------------------------
Totals:  1003
Sum:                                      $ 65.10
-----------------------------------------------------------------


  2001          8114       9115           $ 10.90    06-jun-1989
-----------------------------------------------------------------
Totals:  2001
Sum:                                      $ 10.90
-----------------------------------------------------------------


  3001          8116       9111           $ 29.25    10-may-1989
-----------------------------------------------------------------
Totals:  3001
Sum:                                      $ 29.25
-----------------------------------------------------------------


  4001          8115       9114           $ 73.98    01-sep-1989
-----------------------------------------------------------------
Totals:  4001
Sum:                                      $ 73.98
-----------------------------------------------------------------
=================================================================
Grand Totals:   REPORT
Sum:                                      $ 275.96
=================================================================
```

FIGURE 3.22 *Sales Activity Report Printout*

```
                    INVENTORY STATUS REPORT
              Arizona Widget Wholesale Supply Company
              -------  ------  ---------  ------  -------

                                            Re-
Part No.    Description                Qty   Ordr        Cost
--------    -----------                ---   ----        ----
   9111     wrench                     2000   100     $  1.35
   9112     socket set                  100    20     $ 14.95
   9113     screwdriver, phillips #2    250    50     $   .89
   9114     test meter, m5               60    10     $ 25.50
   9115     pliers, 3 inch             2500   200     $  1.50
===============================================================
Grand Totals:   REPORT

Sum:                                                 $ 44.19
===============================================================
```

FIGURE 3.23   *Inventory Status Report*

Part 3

INGRES MENU
SQL SYSTEM

Chapter 4

INTERACTING WITH INGRES USING THE STRUCTURED QUERY LANGUAGE (SQL)

■■■■ INGRES QUERY LANGUAGES

INGRES supports two languages, QUEL (query language) and SQL (structured query language). INGRES users can define and manipulate data in relational databases by using either of the two relational languages.

The original query language written for INGRES was QUEL. However, in 1986 the American National Standards Institute decided that a standard query language was needed to end confusion and competition among the different query language dialects. SQL was selected as the official standard query language, and was added as a second query language for INGRES.

Adding SQL allowed users who were familiar with QUEL to continue using it as their language of choice, while also offering the standard query language to new customers. In the coming chapters, we will show the syntax and give brief examples of both languages. The choice of which to use is left up to the user.

SQL and QUEL statements can be introduced to the database by several different tools: 1) with the INGRES Interactive Terminal Monitor; 2) used within applications written in high-level languages such as C and Pascal (via Embedded SQL or QUEL); 3) included in applications built with Applications-By-Forms (ABF), a forms-based application development environment within INGRES; or 4) they may be included in report specifications for the INGRES Report Writer.

The coming chapters will show how to access a database using ISQL and IQUEL (the INGRES Interactive Terminal Monitor mode). Chapters 4 and 5 cover the SQL language, while QUEL is discussed in Chapters 6 and 7. After deciding which language to use, choose the appropriate menu choice from the INGRES main menu, or type **ISQL** <**database**> or **IQUEL** <**database**> at the system prompt. "Database" refers to the name of the database you wish to query. Refer to the INGRES system manuals for your version of INGRES if you are having trouble entering into the Interactive Terminal mode.

The examples in the following sections will introduce SQL syntax using the database and tables created in the previous chapters. The syntax for commands in SQL will be shown with examples as they are to be typed into the Interactive Terminal Monitor. To practice using ISQL, the user should type the example statements as they appear in the figures. To execute the statements choose Go or Complete from the menu. After the commands are processed by the database, compare the figures with the results on your screen.

■■■ LEARNING SYNTAX OF SQL

The Interactive Terminal Monitor allows entry and retrieval of data from the database. Figure 4.1 shows the input screen of the Interactive Terminal Monitor for SQL (ISQL). The user types SQL statements in this screen to execute SQL commands, then activates the Go or Complete menu selection by pressing the appropriate key.

The commands are then processed by the INGRES DBMS, and the results are either printed out on paper or displayed on the output screen. The screen in Figure 4.1 shows that the database being queried is named <database_name>. Menu choices are displayed along the bottom of the screen, along with the key definition in parentheses. Pressing **Help** at this point explains the key definitions. The key definitions shown here may not be the same as those displayed by your terminal. If not, consult the online Help for key definitions.

```
Enter SQL  Statements                    Database: <database_name>
 ┌─────────────────────────────────────────────────────────────────┐
 │                                                                   │
 │                                                                   │
 │                                                                   │
 │                                                                   │
 │                                                                   │
 │                                                                   │
 │                                                                   │
 │                                                                   │
 │                                                                   │
 │                                                                   │
 │                                                                   │
 │                                                                   │
 │                                                                   │
 │                                                                   │
 │                                                                   │
 │  Go()    Resume()  Complete()   Blank()    Edit()   File()   >    │
 └─────────────────────────────────────────────────────────────────┘
```

FIGURE 4.1 *ISQL Menu*

The ISQL menu items are as follows:

Go	Sends the SQL commands to the database for processing. The first screen of output is displayed when it is processed by the database. Scroll forward and the remaining pages (if any) will be displayed. (See "Complete.")
Resume	Returns to the output screen to continue viewing the results from a previous request.
Complete	Sends the SQL commands to the database for processing. Does not display any of the results until the entire request is complete and all output has been returned to ISQL. (See "Go.")
Blank	Deletes all the SQL statements from the input screen.
Edit	Allows user to edit the contents of the input screen using the system editor.
File	Displays a submenu to READ or WRITE a file into or from the input screen. WRITE sends the contents of the screen into a file. READ loads a file into the ISQL screen. For both subcommands you will be prompted for the name of the file.
OnError	Allows user to choose how INGRES handles errors in the SQL statements sent. Selecting the Terminate option ends the processing of commands, while selecting Continue allows the remaining statements to be executed.
InsertLine	Inserts a blank line above the current cursor position on the input screen.
DeleteLine	Deletes the line at the current cursor position on the input screen. If there is no current line or only one line, no line will be deleted.
Help	Displays the Help file.
Quit	Exits from ISQL.

Retrieve the SALESPEOPLE table and select **Go** from the menu. The screen shown in Figure 4.2 will appear.

Note that at the top of the screen several statements appear with numbers and greater-than signs. These statements show the user what was read from the input screen. (These statements will be explained in later sections.) The numbers represent line numbers and the greater-than signs indicate the beginning of the query statement. The line number and ">" are not part of the SQL syntax, but only indicate a row in

```
1> select *
2> from salespeople;
3> commit;
```

lname	fname	salesn	salesofc
Johnson	Henry	1001	Phoenix
Castro	Robert	1002	Phoenix
Barton	Jane	1003	Phoenix
Smith	John	2001	Las Vegas
Santos	Clarissa	3001	San Diego
Travis	Randy	4001	El Paso

```
(6 rows)
End of Request
```

FIGURE 4.2 *SALESPEOPLE Table*

the table. If there are errors in the statements sent to the database, it will be noted here. The line numbers help the user locate errors, since line numbers sometimes are referred to in error messages. The asterisk (*) following "select" is the wildcard character interpreted as "all."

To practice sending commands for processing, simply type exactly what is shown after the line number and the greater-than sign, starting with line 1. (The line numbers should not be typed.) If an error is detected, INGRES will notify the user with an error message. The user must then return to the input screen and correct the error before the transaction will execute.

If the table requested is larger than the screen, you may scroll through the results of your query language request by using the scroll keys for your system. Examine the Help screen for Keys if the keys for your system are different than those shown.

The following menu items (already on the screen from the previous retrieve) are available for viewing the output.

Top	Scrolls to the first page of the results.
Bottom	Scrolls to the last page of the results.
File	Saves the results in a file. You will be prompted for a file name. (Note that only the results which have already been read from the database will be written to the file. If you want to save all the output, be sure to select the Bottom command first.)
Help	Displays the Help file.
End	Returns to the input screen of the Interactive Terminal Monitor.

■■■ SQL DATA DEFINITION STATEMENTS

With a query language users can use data definition statements to define data in a relational database. The principle logical data definition statements for SQL are:

CREATE TABLE [table-name]
DROP [table-name]
CREATE VIEW [view-name]
DROP [view-name]

CREATE TABLE STATEMENT

The general format for the CREATE TABLE statement is:

CREATE TABLE table-name
(column-definition [, column-definition] . . .)

"Table-name" refers to the user-selected name for the table to be created. "Column-definition" includes the name of the column, the data type (see Appendix A for a list of SQL data types) to be in the column, width, and a default specification that determines what shall be in the column when no data is present. The column default specifications are defined when the table is created.

The three default specifications are:

WITH NULL
NOT NULL
NOT NULL WITH DEFAULT

Null is a data value used when a value for a column is unknown or is a value that does not apply. Suppose in an inventory table, there was a column created for the delivery date of an item in inventory. Sometimes this information could be important, such as in the delivery date of supplies in stock, and therefore it may be necessary to find if a delivery date has been entered.

If the WITH NULL value is specified for a column, no value is placed in the column and a Null is assigned.

Null is not considered the same as entering a zero, blank, or empty value. Consider again the table on p. 17 containing a column of people's ages first presented in Chapter 2. As you will recall, when the ages are averaged without all the rows being filled in, an inaccurate averaging results. This is because the rows with zeros figure into the equation and incorrectly compute the average. If this column had defaulted to NULL the row containing the null values would be ignored by mathematical operations.

If a default value of zero or blank is to be placed in an empty column, this can be specified with the NOT NULL WITH DEFAULT statement. By specifying NOT NULL WITH DEFAULT, all columns must be filled in with data.

As an example of using the above data definition statements, submitting the CREATE TABLE statements produces no visible result (see Figure 4.3).

When you need to make a correction to your table, sometimes it is necessary to use CREATE TABLE. It is recommended to use NOT NULL. This procedure corresponds to the RETRIEVE INTO. A useful purpose of this procedure would be to retrieve data into a new table when you need to modify the table columns. You would then be able to add or delete as many columns as needed, and this cannot be done from the menu.

INGRES acknowledges that a table has been created conforming to the specified data types and sizes.

The counterpart to CREATE TABLE is DROP [table-name], where "table-name" specifies the name of the table you want to destroy. The command "DROP temp" would erase or eliminate the TEMP table, and all the data in the table, from the database.

CREATE VIEW STATEMENT

Views (or virtual tables) are created using the CREATE VIEW statement. CREATE VIEW is similar in construction to CREATE TABLE. Views are similar to tables in that they appear the same to the user, but unlike tables, views do not store data for each row and column the way tables do. Instead they are representations, or definitions, of data located in one or more tables. In that case, a VIEW statement must refer to columns that already exist in one or more tables. Views will be discussed in more detail later in this chapter.

■ SQL DATA MANIPULATION STATEMENTS

When sending commands that change the data in tables, statements should be organized and submitted as a *transaction*. Transactions can be thought of as complete units, in that they contain all the commands needed to perform an operation to completion. When the commands have all been typed the transaction should be *committed*.

One common example of transaction processing would be to think in terms of a company's inventory control. Suppose you were using an on-line system and the quantities on hand in the inventory were being changed continuously and not all updates were recorded in the database when input. You would have what is called an inconsistent state. This should not be allowed to occur. One of the commands that helps to ensure this processing is **COMMIT**.

```
1>   create table temp
2>
3>        ( partno char(5) not null,
4>        lname char(20)
5>        salesofc char(12) )
```

FIGURE 4.3 *Creating a Table*

The effects of a user's transaction do not become permanent until the transaction is committed. When the transaction is committed all of its effects are written permanently to the database and they become available to other users. After a user has used COMMIT the current transactions cannot be changed. Not using it could affect other users.

There are four data manipulation statements in SQL: SELECT, INSERT, UPDATE, and DELETE. We will discuss these four in this and the next chapter, beginning with simple queries and progressing to more complex join queries and aggregate functions. (ISQL (Interactive Structure Query Language) is a tool for retrieving data that meets your requirements.)

SELECT STATEMENTS

The SELECT command is the primary tool for data manipulation. It retrieves and displays data from a table or tables as specified in the command statement. Its format is shown below:

SELECT [DISTINCT] (target-list)
FROM table [, table] . . .
[WHERE predicate]
[GROUP BY column(s)]
[HAVING predicate]
[ORDER BY columns(s)]

The elements in the SELECT syntax are as follows:

DISTINCT	In some tables there may be duplication of some column items. The DISTINCT option tells SQL to eliminate duplicates from the result of a SELECT statement. In other words, if the table being searched had Partno 11111 listed in five rows, and if the column Partno was selected, it would only be retrieved once.
(target-list)	This is the list of the columns that you wish to retrieve. Each column is listed as follows: TABLENAME.COLUMNNAME. The suffix "all" following the table name will retrieve all of the columns in the table. Multiple columns are separated by a comma.
FROM table	Names the table or tables where data is to be located.
WHERE	This optional phrase allows conditions to be used to limit the retrieval. A typical example might be "WHERE customer.cuscity = 'Phoenix.'" This causes only the columns where the city is stored as "Phoenix" to be retrieved. Any of the normal

	logical operators can be used, such as $=$, $>$, $<$, $<=$, $>=$, $<>$ (!=), AND, OR.
GROUP BY	Specifies the columns that comprise the grouping.
HAVING	Further restricts the data called for in above search condition.
ORDER BY	Allows the user to specify that the retrieval be sorted by one or more columns.

In the examples that follow we will use SELECT to build tables by selecting columns and data from an existing table. These are called *single-table queries* since they select from only one table.

To create the rows in a new table it is necessary to specify what data you want to retrieve, or SELECT, from the existing table. For retrieval of an entire table enter the following command:

select *
from customer;
commit;

The screen shown in Figure 4.4 will appear.

The statement directs the DBMS to display all of the data in the CUSTOMER table. Figure 4.4 shows a table that cannot be viewed completely on the screen. Some of the columns are not visible. Selecting Help and Keys will show you a list of the command keys that will allow you to scroll the table across the screen so that you can see the remaining columns.

Figure 4.5 shows the output screen after another SELECT command has been processed by the DBMS. Type the commands as shown in Figure 4.5 after the line numbers and greater-than symbols. The greater-than symbol is used to point to the beginning of the line.

It is possible to rearrange the rows in any sequence desired, as shown in Figure 4.6. The commands (as indicated with line numbers in Figure 4.6) are typed into the input screen and sent to be processed.

DISTINCT OPTION

The DISTINCT option can be used when a table has duplicate entries in a column and you are only interested in whether the specific data occurs once if at all. For example, the TRANSACTIONS table lists the part number ordered in each transaction. You may wish to know only if the part has been ordered, and not the number of times it has been ordered.

Figure 4.7 illustrates the result when part number is retrieved without the DISTINCT qualifier, and Figure 4.8 shows the result obtained when the qualifier is used.

ORDERING DATA

The ORDER BY option allows the rows of the table to be sorted or rearranged using the value of one or more of the columns. The sorting can be ascending or descending as specified by the user. The default is ascending. We will start by selecting the

```
1> select *
2> from customer
```

cusname	cusaddress	cuscity	cussta	cuszip	cusphone	cusno
Arizona Supply	65 S. Central	Phoenix	Az	85012	602-271-4955	8113
Atlas Supply	1234 W. Thomas	Phoenix	Az	85019	602-235-4311	8111
Desert Vendors	33. N. Outerloop	Las Vegas	Nv	71345	215-333-4111	8114
Ocean Supply	65 Marine Way	San Diego	Ca	24035	591-695-2211	8116
Saguaro Wholesale	351 Highland	Phoenix	Az	85001	602-344-6000	8112
Western Wholesale	2501 Lee Trevino	El Paso	Tx	64311	415-222-6111	8115

```
(6 rows)
End of Request
```

FIGURE 4.4 *CUSTOMER Table*

```
1> select cusno,cusname,cusphone
2> from customer;
3> commit;
```

cusno	cusname	cusphone
8113	Arizona Supply	602-271-4955
8111	Atlas Supply	602-235-4311
8114	Desert Vendors	215-333-4111
8116	Ocean Supply	591-695-2211
8112	Saguaro Wholesale	602-344-6000
8115	Western Wholesale	415-222-6111

```
(6 rows)
End of Request
```

FIGURE 4.5   *Selected CUSTOMER Table*

```
1> select cusname,cusphone,cusno
2> from customer;
3> commit;
```

cusname	cusphone	cusno
Arizona Supply	602-271-4955	8113
Atlas Supply	602-235-4311	8111
Desert Vendors	215-333-4111	8114
Ocean Supply	591-695-2211	8116
Saguaro Wholesale	602-344-6000	8112
Western Wholesale	415-222-6111	8115

```
(6 rows)
End of Request
```

FIGURE 4.6   *Selected CUSTOMER Table with Rearranged Columns*

```
select partno
from transactions;
commit;
```

partno
9111
9114
9113
9112
9115
9111
9114

```
(7 rows)
End of Request
```

FIGURE 4.7   *Selected TRANS-
ACTIONS Table Without DISTINCT
Qualifier*

```
select distinct partno
from transactions;
commit;

  partno

    9111
    9112
    9113
    9114
    9115

(5 rows)
End of Request
```

FIGURE 4.8   *Selected TRANS-
ACTIONS Table with DISTINCT
Qualifier*

columns Salesno, Lname, and Salesofc from the SALESPEOPLE table as it is stored.
See Figure 4.9.

The addition of the ORDER BY clause will allow arranging the same table so that
it is collated according to the last names of the salespeople instead of sales number
order as it was entered. The sort key must be a column that will appear in the resultant
table (Figure 4.10).

A multiple sort can be implemented by using more than one sort key. The column
listed first is the primary sort key. Within the primary sort the rows will be sorted in
accordance with the secondary sort key. See Figure 4.11.

CONDITION STATEMENTS

The WHERE qualifier allows us to retrieve selected records from a table while ignoring all rows that do not meet the conditions that have been defined. The WHERE
qualifier allows the user to ask specific questions about the data without having to

```
1> select salesno,lname,salesofc
2> from salespeople;
3> commit;

 salesn  lname          salesofc

   1001  Johnson        Phoenix
   1002  Castro         Phoenix
   1003  Barton         Phoenix
   2001  Smith          Las Vegas
   3001  Santos         San Diego
   4001  Travis         El Paso

(6 rows)
End of Request
```

FIGURE 4.9   *Selected SALESPEOPLE Table*

```
1> select partno, cusno, date
2> from transactions
3> where partno=9111
4> and cusno=8116
5> and date < '20-feb-89';
6> commit;
```

partno	cusno	date
9111	8116	10-feb-1989

```
(1 rows)
End of Request
```

FIGURE 4.14 *Expanded Search with AND*

The SELECT command searched for all rows in the CUSTOMER table where the customer name was LIKE a string beginning with the letter "A," then an unknown character followed by an "i," then an unknown, then the letter "o" followed by the percent sign (means that any characters can fill in the rest of the blank).

The SELECT command delivers the customer name and customer address columns that fit the search pattern described after the LIKE statement.

When specifying a search condition, as in the WHERE predicate, the proper case for the search qualifier is necessary. The commands in Figure 4.15 specify a search for any sales office that starts with the capital letter "P." If the sales office begins with a lowercase "p" no rows will be found.

DERIVED COLUMNS

So far all of the SELECT examples that have been shown have consisted of tables made up of columns that actually exist in the original stored table. With the SELECT command we can also use derived columns and reference columns to add to the table.

```
1> select lname, salesno, salesofc
2> from salespeople
3> where salesofc like 'P%';
4> commit;
```

lname	salesn	salesofc
Johnson	1001	Phoenix
Castro	1002	Phoenix
Barton	1003	Phoenix

```
(3 rows)
End of Request
```

FIGURE 4.15 *Selected Table Using % Wildcard*

```
1> select partno, price
2> from inventory;
3> commit;
```

partno	price
9111	$1.95
9112	$21.70
9113	$1.30
9114	$36.99
9115	$2.18

```
(5 rows)
End of Request
```

FIGURE 4.16 *Selected INVENTORY Table*

Additionally, column names that appear at the top of each column of the table can be changed in the SELECT statement.

First select the Partno and Price columns from the INVENTORY table and display it as it is stored (Figure 4.16). We will change the titles and add columns that are not in the table.

First change the column heading Partno to ID by typing the statements shown in Figure 4.17.

Now we will add a column that denotes a 12% tax to be applied to the price, and a derived column that will show the price to charge with the tax included. Type in the statements shown in Figure 4.18.

It should be obvious that this ability to add derived columns offers many possi-

```
1> select
2> id=partno,
3> price
4> from inventory;
5> commit;
```

id	price
9111	$1.95
9112	$21.70
9113	$1.30
9114	$36.99
9115	$2.18

```
(5 rows)
End of Request
```

FIGURE 4.17 *Renaming Column Heading*

```
1> select
2> id=partno,
3> price,
4> reference='12% tax',
5> total=price*1.12
6> from inventory;
7> commit;
```

id	price	referen	total
9111	$1.95	12% Tax	$2.18
9112	$21.70	12% Tax	$24.30
9113	$1.30	12% Tax	$1.46
9114	$36.99	12% Tax	$41.43
9115	$2.18	12% Tax	$2.44

```
(5 rows)
End of Request
```

FIGURE 4.18 *Adding Reference and Derived Columns*

bilities for creative uses of your original data. Changing the titles may not appear to add much to the equation, but this can be used to make titles more readable.

■ MORE ON VIEWS

You have learned to use the SELECT command for data manipulation. This statement can also be used for data definition when creating views.

As discussed earlier, views do not store data as tables do, but are representations of data. By using VIEW the user can experiment with different groupings of data from several tables without altering any of the data. Use a sub-select construct to select from one or more tables.

The syntax of the CREATE VIEW statement is:

CREATE VIEW view-name
[(column-name [, column-name] . . .)]
AS sub-select

"View-name" is a user-specified name for the view. "Column-name" specifies the column names from table(s) you wish to view. "AS sub-select" refers to a SELECT statement used as a subcommand to obtain specific data to create the VIEW.

For an example of the CREATE VIEW statement using a sub-select, enter the following commands:

create view tempview (cusname, cusno)
as select customer.cusname, customer.cusno
from customer

The view created appears much the same as a table. The column names specified in the CREATE VIEW statement must exist in the table or tables that the sub-select calls on. See the SELECT command for the correct syntax to use in a sub-select. The sub-select is the same as a SELECT command, but is used along with the CREATE VIEW command to create a logical table from existing tables.

INGRES will acknowledge the creation of the view but will not display it. To see the view that you have created access it as you would a table, most likely using a SELECT command. The sub-select in the CREATE VIEW follows the rules for the SELECT command.

MULTIPLE-TABLE QUERIES

So far we have been selecting data from single tables. One of the powers of a relational database is its ability to work with more than one table at the same time. When two or more tables are addressed by the same query it is called a *join*. The important point in creating a join between tables is that there must exist a common column to establish a link between the tables. This key column can be any of the columns in the table, and can be either alphanumeric or numeric. See Figure 4.19.

For a simple example, suppose a sales manager is viewing the transactions of the last period and wants to see the names as well as the sales numbers of the salespeople responsible for the transactions. The following query, selecting data from the SALESPEOPLE and TRANSACTIONS tables, would satisfy the requirement.

This could be narrowed down to a particular salesperson by adding an AND condition as in Figure 4.20.

```
1> select salespeople.lname, transactions.partno, transactions.cusno,
2>         transactions.date
3> from salespeople, transactions
4> where salespeople.salesno=transactions.salesno;
5> commit;
```

lname	partno	cusno	date
Johnson	9111	8111	20-feb-1989
Johnson	9114	8113	18-feb-1989
Castro	9113	8113	30-jan-1989
Barton	9112	8112	15-feb-1989
Smith	9115	8114	31-jan-1989
Santos	9111	8116	10-feb-1989
Travis	9114	8115	05-feb-1989

```
(7 rows)
End of Request
```

FIGURE 4.19 *A Join Between Two Tables*

```
1> select salespeople.lname, transactions.partno,
2> transactions.cusno, transactions.date
3> from salespeople, transactions
4> where salespeople.salesno=transactions.salesno
5> and salespeople.salesno=1001;
6> commit;
```

lname	partno	cusno	date
Johnson	9111	8111	20-feb-1989
Johnson	9114	8113	18-feb-1989

```
(2 rows)
End of Request
```

FIGURE 4.20   *A Join with an AND Condition*

◼ EXERCISES

1. Design exercises:
   a. Build a table called PATIENTS with the following columns:

   first_name = character 10
   last_name = character 15
   address   = character 20
   city   = character 15
   state   = character 2
   phone   = character 12
   zip   = character 5
   date_mem   = date
   cusid   = integer 2

   b. Insert the following data into the PATIENTS table:

Name	Address	City	State	Phone
Sue Gray	1212 W. Thomas	Phoenix	AZ	602-943-8765
Harry Ford	345 E. Northern	Phoenix	AZ	602-944-2366
George Burns	111 N. 13th Ave	Tucson	AZ	602-345-3210
Sherns Adams	4532 W. Indian	Tucson	AZ	602-465-2349
Ann Wilson	7538 N. Central	Phoenix	AZ	602-945-8877
Majid Rezai	4500 E. Rasht	Chandler	AZ	602-555-6678

Zip	Date	ID
85002	Feb-01-90	1001
85349	Jan-10-90	1002
85610	Mar-09-90	1003
85122	Mar-11-90	1004
85334	Apr-11-90	1005
85444	Jan-05-90	1006

c. Build another table called FEES with the following columns:

```
cusid        = integer 2
fees         = money
date_billed  = date
```

d. Insert the following data into the FEES table:

ID	Fees	Date Billed
1001	$ 55.50	March 10, 1990
1003	75.00	July 10, 1990
1006	100.00	January 01, 1990
1002	43.00	February 02, 1990
1004	67.50	October 10, 1990
1005	80.00	December 12, 1990
1006	75.00	May 05, 1990
1001	89.00	May 05, 1990

e. Build a table called FEESPAID with the following columns:

```
cusid       = integer 2
fees_paid  = money
date_paid  = date
```

f. Insert the following data into the FEESPAID table:

ID	Fees Paid	Date Paid
1004	$ 67.50	November 11, 1990
1001	55.50	April 10, 1990
1002	43.00	March 02, 1990
1006	100.00	February 01, 1990
1003	35.00	August 10, 1990
1001	90.00	May 01, 1990

2. SELECT statement exercises:
   a. Display all the columns from PATIENTS.
   b. Display a subset of columns from PATIENTS.
   c. Display from PATIENTS those from Tucson.

d. Display the patients between the membership dates of January 12, 1990 and June 10, 1990.

e. Display the first name from PATIENTS and sort in ascending order.

f. Display all patients that have fees billed on or before October 10, 1990. Include first_name, fees.cusid, and date_billed.

g. Display city, state, first name, and last name where their fees are greater than or equal to $75.00.

h. Display the first name where the customer identification is greater than or equal to 1002 and less than or equal to 1005.

i. Display those patients that have been billed and have not paid.

j. Display all the columns in the FEES table.

k. Display all the columns in the FEESPAID table.

l. Display PATIENTS and FEES tables together.

m. Display the city, state, first name, and last name where their fees are greater than or equal to $20.00 and less than or equal to $100.00.

n. Display all patients with their fees where patients live in Phoenix.

o. Display patients' identification numbers along with their first names.

Chapter 5

AGGREGATE OPERATORS AND ADDITIONAL SQL STATEMENTS

◼ AGGREGATE OPERATORS

SQL provides special operators, known as *aggregates,* to improve its retrieval functions. They follow the general form of:

aggregate (scalar-expression [WHERE predicate])

The aggregate operators perform mathematical operations on columns. The five basic aggregates are:

COUNT	Returns the number of values in the column.
SUM	Returns the sum of the values in the column.
AVG	Returns the average of the values in the column.
MAX	Returns the largest value in the column.
MIN	Returns the smallest value in the column.

Additional aggregate operators are COUNT [DISTINCT], SUM [DISTINCT], and AVG [DISTINCT]. Operators with "DISTINCT" function similarly to COUNT, SUM, or AVG except that they eliminate duplicate data from the operation.

Since the aggregates perform mathematical functions, the columns that are operated on contain numeric, money, or date/time data types. MAX and MIN can be used with characters.

COUNT

The COUNT aggregate can be used to find the number of rows in a table, as shown in Figure 5.1 below.

```
1> select num_salespeople = count (salesno)
2> from salespeople;
3> commit;

num_salesmen

              6

(1 row)
End of Request
```

FIGURE 5.1 *Using the COUNT Aggregate*

In Figure 5.1 the SELECT command counts the rows in the Salesno column of the SALESPEOPLE table. Then it assigns the value to the Num_salespeople column. Assuming all the rows have sales numbers, the result shows the total number of files in the SALESPEOPLE table.

AVG

To average the numbers in the price column of the INVENTORY table, the statement shown in Figure 5.2 might be issued.

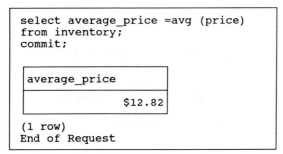

```
select average_price =avg (price)
from inventory;
commit;

average_price

        $12.82

(1 row)
End of Request
```

FIGURE 5.2 *Using the AVG Aggregate*

The AVG (distinct) aggregate will average values in a column excluding all repeated values.

MAX AND MIN

The MAX command as shown in Figure 5.3 will return the largest number in the Qty column of the TRANSACTIONS table.

```
select maxqty = max (qty)
from transactions;
commit;


 maxqty

      15


(1 row)
End of Request
```

FIGURE 5.3   *Using the MAX Aggregate*

For the minimum quantity in the Qty column, type the command shown in Figure 5.4.

```
select minqty = min (qty)
from transactions;
commit;


 minqty

       1


(1 row)
End of Request
```

FIGURE 5.4   *Using the MIN Aggregate*

SUM

To sum all the values in the Qty column of the TRANSACTIONS table, the following command shown in Figure 5.5 can be entered.

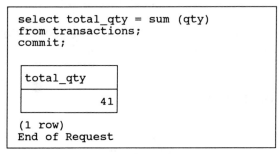

```
select total_qty = sum (qty)
from transactions;
commit;

┌─────────────────────┐
│ total_qty           │
├─────────────────────┤
│                  41 │
└─────────────────────┘

(1 row)
End of Request
```

FIGURE 5.5   *Using the SUM Aggregate*

Compare the use of the SUM aggregate (Figure 5.5) with the SUM (distinct) aggregate (Figure 5.6). The spelling is the option of the user.

```
select total_u_qty = sum   (distinct qty )
from transactions;
commit;

┌─────────────────────┐
│ total_u_qty         │
├─────────────────────┤
│                  36 │
└─────────────────────┘

(1 row)
End of Request
```

FIGURE 5.6   *Using the SUM (Distinct) Aggregate*

With the SUM (distinct) aggregate, all values in the quantity column, excluding repeated values, are added. In the Qty column of the TRANSACTIONS table the number 5 occurs twice. Since that is the only number repeated, the second 5 is not included in the summing operation. Hence the result in Figure 5.6 is five less than the result in Figure 5.5.

Adding the WHERE predicate to the SUM aggregate allows further distillation of data as shown in Figure 5.7.

```
select sum_qty = sum ( qty )
from transactions
where price < 30.00;
commit;

┌─────────────────────┐
│ sum_qty             │
├─────────────────────┤
│                  35 │
└─────────────────────┘

(1 row)
End of Request
```

FIGURE 5.7   *Using SUM with WHERE Condition*

■ ADDITIONAL SQL COMMANDS

In the previous chapter we discussed the SELECT statement. The remaining commands, INSERT, UPDATE, and DELETE, update tables.

INSERT STATEMENT

The INSERT statement has the general form:

> **INSERT INTO table (column [,column] . . .)**
> **VALUES (constant [,constant] . . .) [sub-select]**

> **Table (column)**   Specifies the name of the table and columns that
> the data is to be inserted into.

> **VALUES**   Expressions in VALUES can only be constants
> (including NULL), scalar functions on constants,
> or arithmetic operations on constants.

> **[sub-select]**   A select command added to the INSERT INTO
> command. The sub-select can take the place of a
> VALUES constant.

Either the VALUES clause or the sub-select must appear. See Chapter 4 for a description of the sub-select syntax.

The list of column names after the table name may be omitted if:

a) A sub-select is used and the column names in the sub-select agree with the columns in the table.

b) The expressions specified in the VALUES statement correspond to the columns in the table.

When using INSERT INTO in SQL, a table must first be created. In SQL, unlike QUEL, data cannot be inserted into a table that does not exist. (In QUEL it is possible to insert data into tables that have not been previously created.)

To interact with the following INSERT example, we will first create the PHONE table. Type the statement **create table phone (cusname c25, cusphone c12)** in the input screen of the Interactive ISQL Monitor. After you send the command to be processed by selecting **Go** from the menu, the output screen will acknowledge the request by showing the following statement:

> **create table phone**
>
> **(cusname c25, cusphone c12);**
> **commit;**

To populate the new table, use the INSERT clause as shown in Figure 5.8. By using the SELECT statement with the INSERT statement, the selected data is in-

---

serted into the table. When creating a new table be careful to specify a table name that is not already in use.

```
insert into phone (cusname, cusphone)
select cusname, cusphone
from customer;
commit;

(6 rows)
End of Request
```

FIGURE 5.8   *Using INSERT to Insert Data into Table*

The commands in Figure 5.8 create a new phone list, containing only the customers' names and phone numbers. No table is shown, but the database acknowledges the request.

To retrieve the phone list the following command in Figure 5.9 would be used:

```
select *
from phone;
commit;
```

cusname	cusphone
Arizona Supply	602-271-4955
Atlas Supply	602-235-4311
Desert Vendors	215-333-4111
Ocean Supply	591-695-2211
Saguaro Wholesale	602-344-6000
Western Wholesale	415-222-6111

```
(6 rows)
End of Request
```

FIGURE 5.9   *PHONE Table*

Now we will create a new table called SAMPLE for the examples below. Type in the following statement:

create table sample
(lname c25,
price money,
cusno smallint,
salesno smallint,
salesofc c15);
commit;

1. Add a new row to the SAMPLE table.

   insert into sample (lname, price, cusno, salesno, salesofc)
   values ('Williams', 12.50, 1001, 4001, 'Phoenix');
   commit;

2. Insert into the SAMPLE table all rows from the SALESPEOPLE and TRANS-ACTIONS tables specified in the sub-select statement.

   insert into sample(lname, price, cusno, salesno, salesofc)
   select salespeople.lname, salespeople.price, transactions.cusno,
   salespeople.salesno, salespeople.salesofc
   from salespeople, transactions
   where salespeople.salesno > 1001;
   commit;

3. Insert into the SAMPLE table using default columns:

   insert into sample
   values ('Rourke', 11.95, 1002, 4002, 'New York')

The above commands will add to the table SAMPLE. The table to be added to must contain identical column names as those columns requested (specified in the target list) for inserting. An INSERT statement can only be issued by the owner (creator) of the table, or if the user has insert permission on the table.

UPDATE STATEMENT

The UPDATE statement is used to add new data to a table and has the general form:

UPDATE table
SET column = expression [,column = expression] . . .
WHERE predicate

table	Represents the name of the table that is to be updated.
SET	Contains the new data to put in rows.
WHERE	Limits the update to records specified.

All records that meet the qualifications specified in the WHERE predicate will be replaced with the values specified in the SET list. For example, enter the following:

update sample
set salesofc = 'Phoenix'
where salesno = 1002;
commit;

Submitting the above command will replace the Salesofc information in the SAMPLE table, where Salesno = 1002. The Salesno should now be 1002, and the Salesofc should now be "Phoenix." You may wish to check the table to see your changes. Use the SELECT command to see the table.

DELETE STATEMENT

The final table updating command is DELETE. It has the general form of:

DELETE FROM table
[WHERE predicate]

"Table" indicates the table from which data is to be deleted. "WHERE" limits the DELETE command to operate on specific rows. **CAUTION: Be careful when using DELETE without the WHERE qualifier, as the DELETE command will affect the entire table.**

Single-Row Deletion. The following command will delete any row containing salesno 1002.

delete
from sample
Where salesno = 1002
commit;

Multiple-Row Deletion. The following is an example of a multiple-record deletion.

delete
from sample
Where salesofc = 'Phoenix'
commit;

All rows in the SAMPLE table with "Phoenix" in the Salesofc column will be deleted.

■■ EXERCISES

1. Aggregates exercises:
    a. Using the tables created in the exercises in Chapter 4, display the sum of the patients' fees owed with their customer identification, first name, and last name.
    b. Display the patients' fees received with their first name and address.
    c. Display the maximum amount of the patients' fees with the first name and customer identification.
    d. Display the minimum amount of the patients' fees with the first and last name, and the fee.

e. Display the average fee of the patients' fees.

f. Display the sum of the bills of patients that have not made a payment.

2. INSERT, UPDATE, and DELETE exercises:

a. Add a new patient to the PATIENTS table: Arther Simson, 1200 W. Kearn, Yuma, AZ, 602-856-2299, 85400, May 05, 1990, 1007.

b. Set up his account so that he owes $66.00 on June-06-90.

c. Update Ann Wilson's fees billed to $73.00 on June-12-90.

d. Add George Burns's payment of $40.00 on November 1, 1990.

e. Display the complete statement for George Burns including fees billed and fees paid.

f. Add a new patient: Esmat Asghari, 7501 E. Palo Verde, Scottsdale, AZ, 85250, September 10, 1990, 1008.

g. Set up her account so that she owes $75.00 on Oct-10-90.

h. Add an additional fee of $50.00 to Esmat Asghari's account.

i. Display the total fees of Esmat Asghari's account including her first and last name and her identification number.

j. Display the total of all fees paid.

CASE STUDY

Following is an independent exercise to practice the skills you have learned to this point. This case study tracks telephone extensions in a college. You will be asked to:

- create a database
- create three tables
- enter data into tables
- create queries or reports as desired

One of the goals you must set for yourself is to create as many queries or reports as you can. There are no required ones nor is there one "best" solution.

First, create the database using a name of your choice. The following are the table descriptions you will create:

Department Table

Code	char(2)
Description	varchar(25)

Building Table

Code	char(2)
Description	varchar(25)

Extension Table

Department	char(2)
Building	char(2)
Room	char(4)
Name	varchar(32)
Extension	char(5)
port	char(3)

The following is the data to enter into the tables:

Department Table

01	Business
02	Art
03	Math
04	Physical Education
05	Science
06	English

Building Table

- A Business/English
- B Physical Ed.
- C Math/Science
- D Art/Theater

Extension Table

Dept	Building	Room #	Name	Extension	Port
01	A	B101	Candy Apple	51111	101
01	A	B102	Paul Boxer	51112	102
02	D	D101	George Wood	51113	103
02	D	D102	Paula Axe	51114	104
03	C	C101	Chris Cross	51115	105
03	C	C102	Frank Wright	51116	106
04	B	B201	Riely Zinky	51117	107
04	B	B202	Bob Berke	51118	108
05	C	C201	Carla Olson	51119	109
05	C	C202	Richard Ono	51120	110
06	A	A201	Tarra Fischer	51121	111
06	A	A202	Shelby Usher	51122	112

After you have created the database, created the tables, and entered the data, create several query screens or reports as desired.

Part 4

INGRES MENU
QUEL SYSTEM

Chapter 6

INTERACTIVE WITH QUEL USING THE QUERY LANGUAGE

■■■■ USING THE INTERACTIVE TERMINAL MONITOR

QUEL statements can be introduced to the INGRES database by means of the Interactive Terminal Monitor. The Interactive Terminal Monitor for QUEL (IQUEL) is an interactive interface for executing QUEL statements and viewing the output. Figure 6.1 shows the input screen of IQUEL. Select IQUEL from INGRES menu to access the input screen.

The input screen contains a simple box into which you may type QUEL statements. To execute QUEL statements, select the Go or Complete menu items. After the commands are processed by the DBMS the results will be displayed on the output screen.

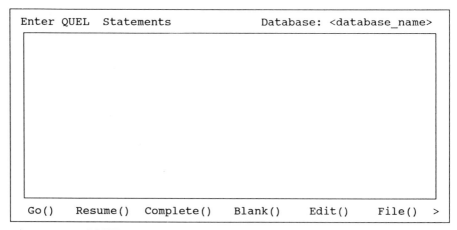

FIGURE 6.1 *IQUEL Menu*

The IQUEL menu choices are as follows:

Go   Sends the QUEL commands to the database for execution. The first screen of output will be displayed when it is processed by the database. As you scroll forward the remaining pages will be displayed. (See ''Complete.'')

Resume   Returns to the output screen to continue viewing the results from a previous request.

Complete   Sends the QUEL statements to the database for execution. Does not display any of the results until the entire request is complete and all output has been returned to IQUEL. (See ''Go.'')

Blank   Deletes all the QUEL statements from the input screen.

Edit   Allows user to edit the contents of the input screen using the system editor.

File   Displays a submenu to READ or WRITE a file into or from the input screen. WRITE sends the contents of the input screen into a file. READ loads a file into the ISQL screen. For both subcommands you will be prompted for the name of the file.

OnError   Displays a pop-up form indicating what will happen if an error is encountered on one of your QUEL statements. Selecting Terminate ends the processing of these statements, while selecting Continue allows the remaining statements to be executed. You may change this option by selecting the appropriate setting.

InsertLine   Inserts a blank line above the current cursor position in the input screen.

DeleteLine   Deletes the line at the current cursor position in the input table column. If there is no current line or only one line, no line will be deleted.

Help   Displays Help file.

Quit   Exits from IQUEL.

Shown below (Figure 6.2) is an example of the Interactive Terminal Monitor screen after the statement **print salespeople** is typed onto the screen and the **Go** command is selected from the menu. The command is processed and the output screen appears in which you may scroll through the results of your query language request.
Scroll forwards or backwards using the **Scrolldown** and **Scrollup** keys defined in

the Key Definition File. Scroll left or right using the **Scrollleft** and **Scrollright** keys. Examine Help for Keys in the Help menu if you need to know the current key definitions for your system.

```
print salespeople

  lname                    fname            salesn  salesofc

  Johnson                  Henry              1001  Phoenix
  Castro                   Robert             1002  Phoenix
  Barton                   Jane               1003  Phoenix
  Smith                    John               2001  Las Vegas
  Santos                   Clarissa           3001  San Diego
  Travis                   Randy              4001  El Paso

(6 rows)
End of Request
```

FIGURE 6.2 *SALESPEOPLE Table*

In addition, the following IQUEL menu items are available for viewing the output:

Top	Scrolls to the first page of the results.
Bottom	Scrolls to the last page of the results.
File	Saves the results in a file. You will be prompted for a file name. (Note that only the results that have already been read from the database will be written to the file. If you want to save all the output, be sure to select the Bottom command first to be sure that all of the data requested has been retrieved from the database.)
Help	Displays this Help file.
End	Returns to the input screen of the Interactive Terminal Monitor.

■ QUEL DATA DEFINITION STATEMENTS

Users can use data definition statements with a query language to define data in a relational database. The principle logical data definition statements for QUEL are:

CREATE (base-table)
DESTROY (base-table)

DEFINE (view)
DESTROY (view)

CREATE STATEMENT

The CREATE statement creates a table, much as discussed in the SQL chapter. The general format for the CREATE statement is:

CREATE base-table
(column-definition [, column-definition] . . .)

"Base-table" refers to the name the user has selected for the table to be created. "Column-definition" takes the form:

column = data-type [default-spec]

Columns for the table are assigned the appropriate length and data type (see Appendix B for a complete listing of data types). "Default-spec" refers to default specifications and may be one of the following:

WITH NULL
NOT NULL
NOT NULL WITH DEFAULT

The optional "default-specs" are similar to those for the CREATE command in SQL (see the section "CREATE TABLE Statement" in Chapter 4).

An example of the CREATE statement is:

CREATE temp
    (partno = char(5) not null,
    lname = char(20),
    salesofc = char(12))

The above command produces the screen shown in Figure 6.3.

```
create temp
   (partno = char(5) not null,
    lname = char(20),
    salesofc = char(12) )
```

FIGURE 6.3 *Creating a Table*

A table has been created with columns conforming to the specified data types and sizes. There is, however, no data in the table.

The counterpart to CREATE table is DESTROY table. An example of the DESTROY statement is:

DESTROY temp

The above command would erase, or eliminate, the TEMP table from the database.

The DEFINE (view) and DESTROY (view) commands operate much as the CREATE VIEW and DROP VIEW commands for the SQL query language.

◼◼ QUEL DATA MANIPULATION STATEMENTS

There are four data manipulation statements in QUEL. They are RETRIEVE, APPEND, REPLACE, and DELETE. We will discuss these four in this and the next chapter, beginning with simple queries and then progressing to the more complex join queries, aggregates, and aggregate functions. (A *query* is a tool for retrieving data that meets your requirements.)

RETRIEVE COMMAND

The RETRIEVE command is the primary tool for data manipulation. It retrieves and displays data from a table or tables as specified in the command statement. Its format is shown below:

> **RETRIEVE [INTO table] [UNIQUE] (target-list)**
> **[WHERE predicate]**
> **[SORT BY column(s)]**

The meaning of the various components of the command are explained briefly below. They will be explained in more detail as they are used later on in the chapter.

INTO table	Allows you to put the data into a new table as opposed to viewing it on the screen.
UNIQUE	In some tables there may be repeats of key column items. The UNIQUE option tells INGRES to eliminate the duplicates. In other words, if the table being searched had partno 11111 listed in five rows, it would be displayed only once.
(target-list)	The list of columns you wish to retrieve. Each column is listed as follows: TABLENAME.column-NAME. The suffix "all" following the table name will retrieve all of the columns in the table. Multiple columns are separated by a comma.
WHERE predicate	This optional phrase allows conditions to be used to limit the retrieval. A typical example might be: WHERE customer.cuscity = "Phoenix." This causes only the columns where the city is stored as "Phoenix" to be retrieved. Any of the normal logical operators can be used, such as =, >, <, < =, > =, < >(! =), AND, OR.
SORT BY column(s)	Allows the user to specify that the retrieval be sorted by one or more columns.

In the examples that follow we will use RETRIEVE to build tables by selecting columns and data from an existing table. These are called *single-table queries* since they retrieve data from only one table.

We will start with a simple version of the RETRIEVE command: the retrieval of an entire table. Type the command as shown at the top of Figure 6.4. The table below it represents the screen output that you should see as a result of entering the commands.

```
retrieve (customer.all)
```

cusname	cusaddress	cuscity	cussta	cuszip	cusphone	cusno
Arizona Supply	65 S. Central	Phoenix	Az	85012	602-271-4955	8113
Atlas Supply	1234 W. Thomas	Phoenix	Az	85019	602-235-4311	8111
Desert Vendors	33. N. Outerloop	Las Vegas	Nv	71345	215-333-4111	8114
Ocean Supply	65 Marine Way	San Diego	Ca	24035	591-695-2211	8116
Saguaro Wholesale	351 Highland	Phoenix	Az	85001	602-344-6000	8112
Western Wholesale	2501 Lee Trevino	El Paso	Tx	64311	415-222-6111	8115

```
(6 rows)
End of Request
```

FIGURE 6.4 *CUSTOMER Table*

This command displays all of the columns in the CUSTOMER table. Figure 6.4 accurately represents the screen, in that all of the columns of the table are not visible. Selecting Help and Keys will show you a list of the command keys that will allow you to scroll the table across the screen so that you can see the remaining columns.

When printed the entire table is visible. However, usually only some columns are selected from the table, and the screen width suffices. The command structure for retrieving selected data would look like:

**RETRIEVE (customer.cusno, customer.cusname,
customer.cusphone)**

The columns that are to be retrieved are specified within the parentheses, with first the table name and then the column name (separated by a period) stated.

Enter the above commands. Now only the requested columns appear on the screen, as shown in Figure 6.5.

```
retrieve (customer.cusno, customer.cusname,
          customer.cusphone

| cusno | cusname           | cusphone     |
|-------|-------------------|--------------|
|  8113 | Arizona Supply    | 602-271-4955 |
|  8111 | Atlas Supply      | 602-235-4311 |
|  8114 | Desert Vendors    | 215-333-4111 |
|  8116 | Ocean Supply      | 591-695-2211 |
|  8112 | Saguaro Wholesale | 602-344-6000 |
|  8115 | Western Wholesale | 415-222-6111 |

(6 rows)
End of Request
```

FIGURE 6.5   *Selecting Table Columns with RETRIEVE*

It is possible to rearrange the columns in any sequence that you desire.

```
retrieve (customer.cusname, customer.cusphone,
          customer.cusno)

| cusname           | cusphone     | cusno |
|-------------------|--------------|-------|
| Arizona Supply    | 602-271-4955 |  8113 |
| Atlas Supply      | 602-235-4311 |  8111 |
| Desert Vendors    | 215-333-4111 |  8114 |
| Ocean Supply      | 591-695-2211 |  8116 |
| Saguaro Wholesale | 602-344-6000 |  8112 |
| Western Wholesale | 415-222-6111 |  8115 |

(6 rows)
End of Request
```

FIGURE 6.6   *Retrieving Columns in a Different Sequence*

UNIQUE COMMAND

The UNIQUE option can be used when a table has duplicate entries of an item and you are only interested in whether the item is present or not. For example, the TRANSACTIONS table lists the part number ordered in each row of the table. You may wish to know only if the part has been ordered, and not the number of times it has been ordered. When UNIQUE is used, repeated values are not displayed.

Figure 6.7 illustrates the part number retrieve without the UNIQUE qualifier, and Figure 6.8, the difference when the qualifier is used.

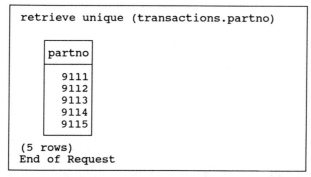

```
retrieve (transactions.partno)

    ┌────────┐
    │ partno │
    ├────────┤
    │   9111 │
    │   9114 │
    │   9113 │
    │   9112 │
    │   9115 │
    │   9111 │
    │   9114 │
    └────────┘

(7 rows)
End of Request
```

FIGURE 6.7   *RETRIEVE Without UNIQUE Qualifier*

```
retrieve unique (transactions.partno)

    ┌────────┐
    │ partno │
    ├────────┤
    │   9111 │
    │   9112 │
    │   9113 │
    │   9114 │
    │   9115 │
    └────────┘

(5 rows)
End of Request
```

FIGURE 6.8   *RETRIEVE with UNIQUE Qualifier*

SORTING DATA

The SORT BY option allows the rows of the table to be sorted or rearranged using the value of one or more of the columns. The sort can be ascending or descending as specified by the user. We will start by selecting columns from the SALESPEOPLE table as shown in Figure 6.9. **NOTE: Ascending is the default and descending must be typed in.**

```
retrieve (salespeople.salesno, salespeople.lname,
          salespeople.salesofc)
```

salesn	lname	salesofc
1001	Johnson	Phoenix
1002	Castro	Phoenix
1003	Barton	Phoenix
2001	Smith	Las Vegas
3001	Santos	San Diego
4001	Travis	El Paso

```
(6 rows)
End of Request
```

FIGURE 6.9   *Selected SALESPEOPLE Table*

The addition of the SORT BY clause will allow us to arrange the same table so that it is collated according to the last name of the salespeople instead of sales number order as it was entered. The sort key must be a column that will appear in the resultant table.

```
retrieve (salespeople.salesno, salespeople.lname,
          salespeople.salesofc)
sort by lname
```

salesn	lname	salesofc
1003	Barton	Phoenix
1002	Castro	Phoenix
1001	Johnson	Phoenix
3001	Santos	San Diego
2001	Smith	Las Vegas
4001	Travis	El Paso

```
(6 rows)
End of Request
```

FIGURE 6.10   *Selected SALESPEOPLE Table Sorted by Last Name*

A multiple sort can be implemented by using more than one sort key. The column listed first is the primary sort key, and within the primary sort the rows will be sorted in accordance with the secondary sort key. See Figure 6.11.

```
retrieve (salespeople.salesno, salespeople.lname,
          salespeople.salesofc)
sort by salesofc, lname
```

salesn	lname	salesofc
1003	Barton	Phoenix
1002	Castro	Phoenix
1001	Johnson	Phoenix
3001	Santos	San Diego
2001	Smith	Las Vegas
4001	Travis	El Paso

```
(6 rows)
End of Request
```

FIGURE 6.11 *Multiple Sort*

CONDITION STATEMENTS

The WHERE condition allows us to retrieve selected rows from a table while ignoring all rows that do not meet the conditions that have been defined. This tool allows the user to answer specific questions about the data without having to look at extra data.

The WHERE condition can be as simple as a search for a row that "equals" certain criteria, such as that shown in Figure 6.12. Or the condition can be as complex as a string of logical phrases that describe which pieces of data are to be retrieved. (The AND operator specifies that two conditions must be met; the OR operator states that either or both of the conditions must be met.) We will use the TRANSACTIONS table for a few examples of the WHERE option.

```
retrieve (transactions.partno, transactions.cusno,
          transactions.date)
where transactions.partno=9111
```

partno	cusno	date
9111	8111	20-feb-1989
9111	8116	10-feb-1989

```
(2 rows)
End of Request
```

FIGURE 6.12 *Simple Search Condition with WHERE*

We can expand this search with an OR condition to pick up not only part number 9111, but also any orders by customer number 8113.

```
retrieve (transactions.partno, transactions.cusno,
          transactions.date)
where transactions.partno = 9111
or transactions.cusno = 8113
```

partno	cusno	date
9111	8111	20-feb-1989
9114	8113	18-feb-1989
9113	8113	30-jan-1989
9111	8116	10-feb-1989

```
(4 rows)
End of Request
```

FIGURE 6.13 *Expanded Search with OR*

The AND condition can be added to further restrict the selected data to that ordered before March 1, 1989.

```
retrieve (transactions.partno, transactions.cusno,
          transactions.date)
where transactions.partno = 9111
or transactions.cusno = 8113
and transactions.date < "1-Mar-89"
```

partno	cusno	date
9111	8116	10-feb-1989

```
(1 rows)
End of Request
```

FIGURE 6.14 *Expanded Search with AND*

INTO STATEMENT

If the user wants to make a permanent row of one of the temporary retrieve tables, the INTO clause can be used. This creates a new table and places the retrieved data into the new table. Be careful to specify a table name that is not already in use.

Enter the following command to make a new phone list of customers sorted by last name.

retrieve into phone (customer.cusname, customer.cusphone)
sort by cusname

No table is shown.

Then, to retrieve the phone list use the command as shown below:

```
retrieve (phone.all)
```

cusname	cusphone
Arizona Supply	602-271-4955
Atlas Supply	602-235-4311
Desert Vendors	215-333-4111
Ocean Supply	591-695-2211
Saguaro Wholesale	602-344-6000
Western Wholesale	415-222-6111

```
(6 rows)
End of Request
```

FIGURE 6.15   *PHONE Table*

Wildcard Searches.   Another capability of INGRES QUEL is the use of wildcard search characters. A wildcard is a character or characters that represent a greater set of characters. For example, the DOS command, DIR *.DOC, asks the computer to search all the files stored on a disk and find any files that end in a suffix of DOC. The asterisk in the command is the wildcard character that stands for any string of characters. The asterisk has the same meaning in INGRES.

The list of acceptable wildcards and what they stand for are:

*	Any sequence of characters.
?	Any single character.
[abc]	Where "abc" is any set of characters in the string "abc. . .".

To see an example of wildcard use, enter the following command:

retrieve (salesmen.lname, salesmen.salesno)
where salesmen.salesofc = "P*"

Normally a distinction between upper- or lowercase is not recognized by INGRES when processing QUEL commands. However, when specifying a search condition, as in the WHERE predicate, you must enter the search qualifier in the proper case.

The program would return a table as in Figure 6.16 displaying all salespeople who work out of any sales office that starts with the capital letter "P." Sales offices that begin with a lowercase "p" will be skipped.

```
retrieve (salespeople.lname,salespeople.salesno)
where salespeople.salesofc="P*"

 lname                          | salesn
 Johnson                        |  1001
 Castro                         |  1002
 Barton                         |  1003

(3 rows)
End of Request
```

FIGURE 6.16 *Search Condition with Wildcard*

CREATING DERIVED COLUMNS
AND CHANGING COLUMN NAMES

So far all of the retrievals that have been shown have consisted of tables made up of columns that actually exist in the original stored table. In the RETRIEVE command we can also use derived columns (new columns) and reference columns (columns from the original table) to add to the table. Additionally, column names that appear at the top of each column of the table can be changed in the RETRIEVE statement.

First select the Partno and Price columns from the INVENTORY table and then display it as it is stored (Figure 6.17). We will make changes to the titles and add columns.

```
retrieve (inventory.partno, inventory.price)

 partno | price
  9111  |        $1.95
  9112  |       $21.70
  9113  |        $1.30
  9114  |       $36.99
  9115  |        $2.18

(5 rows)
End of Request
```

FIGURE 6.17 *Selected INVENTORY Table*

First change the column heading Partno to ID by typing the statements shown in Figure 6.18.

```
retrieve (ID=inventory.partno,inventory.price)

| id   | price   |
|------|---------|
| 9111 |  $1.95  |
| 9112 | $21.70  |
| 9113 |  $1.30  |
| 9114 | $36.99  |
| 9115 |  $2.18  |

(5 rows)
End of Request
```

FIGURE 6.18   *Changing Column Name*

Now add a reference column that denotes that there is a 12% tax to be applied to the price, and a derived column that will show the price to charge with the tax included. See Figure 6.19 for the commands to use.

```
retrieve (ID=inventory.partno, inventory.price,
    reference="12% tax", TOTAL=inventory.price * 1.12)

| id   | price   | referen | total   |
|------|---------|---------|---------|
| 9111 |  $1.95  | 12% tax |  $2.18  |
| 9112 | $21.70  | 12% tax | $24.30  |
| 9113 |  $1.30  | 12% tax |  $1.46  |
| 9114 | $36.99  | 12% tax | $41.43  |
| 9115 |  $2.18  | 12% tax |  $2.44  |

(5 rows)
End of Request
```

FIGURE 6.19   *Adding Reference and Derived Columns*

It should be obvious that this ability to add reference and derived columns offers many possibilities for creative uses of your original data.

■ MULTIPLE-TABLE QUERIES

So far we have been retrieving data from single tables. One of the powers of a relational database is its ability to work with more than one table of data at the same time. When two or more tables are addressed by the same query it is called a *join*. The important point in creating a join between tables is that there must exist a common column that can be used as a key to establish a link between the tables. This key column can be any of the columns in the table, and can be either alphanumeric or numeric.

For a simple example, suppose that a sales manager is viewing the transactions of the last period and wants to see the names as well as the sales numbers of the salespeople responsible for the transactions. The following query, retrieving data from the SALESPEOPLE and TRANSACTIONS tables, would satisfy the requirement.

```
retrieve (salespeople.lname, transactions.partno,
          transactions.cusno, transactions.date)
where salespeople.salesno=transactions.salesno
```

lname	partno	cusno	date
Johnson	9111	8111	20-feb-1989
Castro	9113	8113	30-jan-1989
Barton	9112	8112	15-feb-1989
Smith	9115	8114	31-jan-1989
Santos	9111	8116	10-feb-1989
Travis	9114	8115	05-feb-1989

```
(6 rows)
End of Request
```

FIGURE 6.20 *A Join Between Two Tables*

This could be narrowed down to a particular salesperson by adding an AND condition.

```
retrieve (salespeople.lname, transactions.partno,
          transactions.cusno, transactions.date)
where salespeople.salesno=transactions.salesno
and salespeople.salesno=1001
```

lname	partno	cusno	date
Johnson	9111	8111	20-feb-1989

```
(1 row)
End of Request
```

FIGURE 6.21 *A Join with an AND Condition*

▬▬ EXERCISES

1. Design exercises:
    a. Build a table called PATIENTS with the following columns:

    first_name = character 10
    last_name   = character 15
    address   = character 20
    city   = character 15

state	= character 2
phone	= character 12
zip	= character 5
date_mem	= date
cusid	= integer 2

b. Insert the following data into the PATIENTS table:

Name	Address	City	State	Phone
Sue Gray	1212 W. Thomas	Phoenix	AZ	602-943-8765
Harry Ford	345 E. Northern	Phoenix	AZ	602-944-2366
George Burns	111 N. 13th Ave	Tucson	AZ	602-345-3210
Sherns Admas	4532 W. Indian	Tucson	AZ	602-465-2349
Ann Wilson	7538 N. Central	Phoenix	AZ	602-945-8877
Majid Rezai	4500 E. Rasht	Chandler	AZ	602-555-6678

Zip	Date	ID
85002	Feb-01-90	1001
85349	Jan-10-90	1002
85610	Mar-09-90	1003
85122	Mar-11-90	1004
85334	Apr-11-90	1005
85444	Jan-05-90	1006

c. Build another table called FEES with the following columns:

cusid	= integer 2
fees	= money
date_billed	= date

d. Insert the following data into the FEES table:

ID	Fees	Date_Billed
1001	$ 55.50	March 10, 1990
1003	75.00	July 10, 1990
1006	100.00	January 01, 1990
1002	43.00	February 02, 1990
1004	67.50	October 10, 1990
1005	80.00	December 12, 1990
1006	75.00	May 05, 1990
1001	89.00	May 05, 1990

e. Build a table called FEESPAID with the following columns:

cusid   = integer 2
fees_paid = money
date_paid = date

f. Insert the following data into the FEESPAID table:

ID	Fees Paid	Date Paid
1004	$ 67.50	November 11, 1990
1001	55.50	April 10, 1990
1002	43.00	March 02, 1990
1006	100.00	February 01, 1990
1003	35.00	August 10, 1990
1001	90.00	May 01, 1990

2. RETRIEVE statement exercises:
   a. Display all the columns from PATIENTS.
   b. Display a subset of columns from PATIENTS.
   c. Display from PATIENTS those from Tucson.
   d. Display the patients between the membership dates of January 12, 1990 and June 10, 1990.
   e. Display the first name from PATIENTS and sort in ascending order.
   f. Display all patients that have fees billed on or before October 10, 1990. Include first_name, fees.cusid, and date_billed.
   g. Display city, state, first name, and last name where their fees are greater than or equal to $75.00.
   h. Display the first name where the customer identification is greater than or equal to 1002 and less than or equal to 1005.
   i. Display all the columns in the FEES table.
   j. Display all the columns in the FEESPAID table.
   k. Display PATIENTS and FEES tables together.
   l. Display the city, state, first name, and last name where their fees are greater than or equal to $20.00 and less than or equal to $100.00.
   m. Display all patients with their fees where patients live in Phoenix.
   n. Display patients' identification numbers along with their first names.

Chapter 7

AGGREGATE OPERATORS AND ADDITIONAL QUEL COMMANDS

AGGREGATE OPERATORS

QUEL provides special operators, known as *aggregates,* to improve its retrieval functions. They follow the form of:

aggregate (scalar-expression [WHERE predicate])

There are five basic aggregates:

COUNT	Returns the number of values in the column.
SUM	Returns the sum of the values in the column.
AVG	Returns the average of the values in the column.
MAX	Returns the largest value in the column.
MIN	Returns the smallest value in the column.

Additional aggregate operators are COUNTU, SUMU, and AVGU where the trailing "U" stands for UNIQUE. The operators function similarly to COUNT, SUM, and AVG except that they eliminate duplicate data from the operation (similar to the UNIQUE qualifier for RETRIEVE and APPEND).

Since the aggregates perform mathematical functions, they require that the columns that are operated on contain numeric, money, or date/time data types. Examples of the various aggregate operators follow.

COUNT

The COUNT aggregate can be used to find the number of rows in a table. If you enter the following:

retrieve (num_salespeople = count (salespeople.salesno))

The program will return the data as shown in Figure 7.1.

```
retrieve (num_salespeople=count(salespeople.salesno))

 num_salespeople

             6

(1 row)
End of Request
```

FIGURE 7.1 *Using the COUNT Aggregate*

The preceding command shows that there are a total of six rows in the Salesno column of the SALESPEOPLE table. Assuming all of the rows have sales numbers, the result shows the total number of files in the SALESPEOPLE table.

AVG

To average the numbers in the Price column of the INVENTORY table, the statement shown in Figure 7.2 might be issued.

```
retrieve ( average_price = avg (inventory.price ))

 average_price

        $12.82

(1 row)
End of Request
```

FIGURE 7.2 *Using the AVG Aggregate*

The AVGU (average with UNIQUE) aggregate will average values in a column excluding all repeated values.

MAX and MIN

The MAX command as shown in Figure 7.3 will return the largest number in the Qty column of the TRANSACTION table.

```
retrieve (maxqty = max (transactions.qty))

maxqty

      15

(1 row)
End of Request
```

FIGURE 7.3   *Using the MAX Aggregate*

For the minimum quantity in the Qty column, type the command shown in Figure 7.4.

```
retrieve (minqty = min (transactions.qty))

minqty

     1

(1 row)
End of Request
```

FIGURE 7.4   *Using the MIN Aggregate*

SUM

To sum all the values in the Qty column of the TRANSACTIONS table, the following command can be entered.

```
retrieve (total_qty = sum (transactions.qty))

total_qty

         41

(1 row)
End of Request
```

FIGURE 7.5   *Using the SUM Aggregate*

Compare the use of the SUM aggregate with the SUMU command issued below:

retrieve (total _ u _ qty = sumu (transactions.qty))

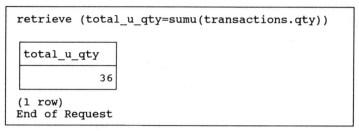

```
retrieve (total_u_qty=sumu(transactions.qty))

    total_u_qty

              36

(1 row)
End of Request
```

FIGURE 7.6 *Using the SUMU Aggregate*

The values in the quantity column, excluding repeated values, are added. In the Qty column of the TRANSACTIONS table, the number 5 occurs twice. The second 5 is not included in the summing operation, so the result (Figure 7.6) is five less than the previous table (Figure 7.5).

Adding the WHERE predicate to the SUM aggregate allows further distillation of data.

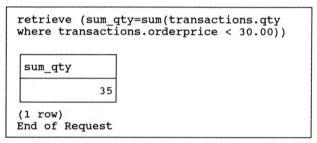

```
retrieve (sum_qty=sum(transactions.qty
where transactions.orderprice < 30.00))

    sum_qty

         35

(1 row)
End of Request
```

FIGURE 7.7 *Using SUM with Condition*

Commands can be further combined. In Figure 7.8 a command is issued that requests a display of all sales numbers from the SALESPEOPLE table that are less than the largest sales number in the column.

```
retrieve ( salespeople.salesno )
where transactions.qty < max (transactions.qty)

    salesno

    1001
    1001
    1002
    1003
    2001
    4001

(6 rowr)
End of Request
```

FIGURE 7.8 *A Condition with MAX*

■ ADDITIONAL QUEL COMMANDS

To continue with the following examples you will need to create a table named SAMPLE. (See CREATE table name, discussed at the beginning of the chapter.) To create the SAMPLE table in QUEL, enter the following command:

```
create sample
(lname = char (20),
partno = char (5) NOT NULL,
cusno = char (5),
salesofc = char (12))
```

In the previous chapter we discussed the RETRIEVE command. The remaining commands, APPEND, REPLACE, and DELETE, update tables.

APPEND COMMAND

The APPEND statement has the general form:

APPEND TO table [UNIQUE] (target-list) [WHERE predicate]

table	Indicates the name of the table that the target-list is to be appended to.
target-list	The list of columns you wish to append. Performs similarly to its function in the RETRIEVE statement.
WHERE	The predicate performs as it does in the RETRIEVE statement explained earlier.

As an example of the APPEND command, enter the following:

append to sample (salespeople.lname, salespeople.partno,
**   transactions.cusno, salespeople.salesofc)**
where salespeople.salesno > 1001

The APPEND command will add to the SAMPLE table (not deleting any rows that happen to be in the SAMPLE table) rows from the specified columns of the tables listed. The table you are adding the data to must have the same column names as the columns requested from the other tables specified in the target-list.

REPLACE COMMAND

The REPLACE statement has the general form:

REPLACE range-variable (target-list) [WHERE predicate]

range-variable	This variable may be a table name.
target-list	Specifies the data that will be replacing the old data.
WHERE	Qualifies where data will be replaced with the values specified in the target list.

Single-Row Replace. The following is an example of a single-row replace.

```
replace sample (salesno = 1001,
salesofc = "Phoenix")
where sample.salesno = 1002
```

The above command will search the SAMPLE table and replace the salesno and salesofc information already in the table with the data specified in the target list, only where salesno = 1002.

Multiple-Row Replace. The following is an example of a multiple-record replace.

```
replace sample (salesofc = "Phoenix")
where sample.salesno = salespeople.salesno
and salespeople.partno > 9111
```

Here the command replaces the information in the Salesofc column in every case where the WHERE and AND qualifiers are true.

DELETE COMMAND

The final table updating command is DELETE. It has the general form of:

DELETE range-variable [WHERE predicate]

As with the REPLACE command, the "range-variable" can be previously declared, or may be a table name. **CAUTION: Be careful when using DELETE without the WHERE qualifier, as the DELETE command will affect the entire table.**

Single-Row Deletion. The following command will delete any row containing salesno 1002.

delete sample where salesno = 1002

Multiple-Row Deletion. The following is an example of a multiple-record deletion.

delete sample where sample.salesofc = "Phoenix"

All rows in the SAMPLE table where salesofc = "Phoenix" will be deleted.

Part 5

ABF COMPONENTS

Chapter 8

INTRODUCTION TO ABF

Applications-By-Forms (ABF) is an INGRES subsystem used to create custom applications. An *application* is an ABF component (in INGRES terminology, an object) typically used to insert, update, delete, and view data in a database. A database can have one or more applications that are used to manipulate data in the database. Before an application can be created in ABF, the database and its tables must first be created.

An application is comprised of components (objects) called frames and procedures. A *frame* is an object that associates a data input screen with a source code (Figure 8.1). The data input screen is called a *form* while the source code is a computer program typically written using INGRES 4GL (fourth-generation language), but may be written using a third-generation language like COBOL, Pascal, FORTRAN, or C.

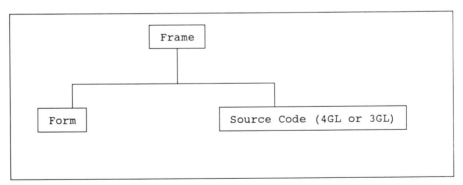

FIGURE 8.1   *Frames Chart*

A *procedure* is source code without a form associated with it (Figure 8.2). A procedure can be written in 4GL or 3GL and is used to perform a function or calculation.

A procedure is similar to a subroutine in that it may be called by more than one frame. The sample application in Chapter 10 will use only INGRES 4GL.

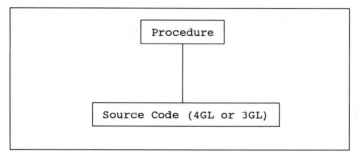

FIGURE 8.2   *Procedure Chart*

INGRES APPLICATIONS AND QUERY LANGUAGES

An INGRES application uses query languages to access a database. An ABF application can use SQL and/or QUEL, although only one language must be defined as the application default language. This means that the SQL and QUEL statements covered in Chapters 4 through 7 are the same statements used in an ABF application to manipulate data. The sample application in this and the next chapter will use SQL.

INGRES APPLICATIONS AND OTHER INGRES SUBSYSTEMS

By using the "call" statement, other INGRES subsystems can be invoked from an application. Although there are many INGRES subsystems that can be called from an application, the most frequently used are Visual-Graphics-Editor (rungraph) to generate graphs and charts, Query-By-Forms (QBF) to query or maintain database tables, and Report Writer (report) to create reports.

INGRES APPLICATIONS AND 4GL

An application can be written using only INGRES 4GL code. INGRES 4GL code differs from standard 3GL in that the code is event driven. For example, the code is modular and based on events that should occur when a user presses a certain key or leaves a particular field on the form. Thus a 4GL program contains fewer lines of code, is easier to understand for maintenance purposes, and is simpler to enhance. Additionally, much of the screen handling is built into INGRES. Functions like field scroll (vertical), table scroll (horizontal), and screen scroll (vertical and horizontal) are built-in. There is no need to write additional code to perform these functions.

ADVANTAGES OF INGRES APPLICATIONS

ABF provides a productive environment to create applications because of these features:

- Code manager keeps track of the source code and compiles only the source code that has changed, thus eliminating the need to remember what needs to be compiled.
- Provides an interpreter for a faster test environment using the Go option.
- Allows testing of specific isolated frames/procedures.
- Typically requires fewer lines of code than 3GL.
- Easier to maintain and enhance.

Chapter 9

INGRES APPLICATIONS AND 4GL

In this chapter INGRES application terminology and 4GL syntax are explained. Then in Chapter 10 we will use the terminology and 4GL to create an application. Figure 9.1 shows a structure chart for the application named "Sample" that you will create in the next chapter.

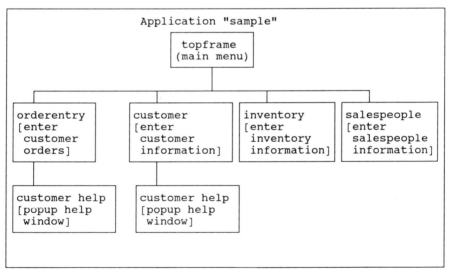

FIGURE 9.1 *Application "Sample" Chart*

Each box in Figure 9.1 represents an application frame. As discussed in Chapter 8, a frame is an application component (object) that has a data input screen called a form and source code that defines the frame's functions (Figure 9.2). For example, "topframe" is the application's main menu. It has a VIFRED form called topframe and an INGRES 4GL program called topframe.osq.

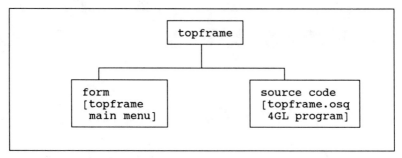

FIGURE 9.2 *Topframe Chart*

FORM STATEMENTS

An INGRES form is a component (object) of a frame that defines what the data input screen looks like. It is created using VIFRED, the Visual-Forms-Editor. A form can display one row at a time or may display multiple rows. The application called "Sample" in Chapter 10 uses both types of forms. Form statements permit data to display on a form, determine when validations occur, display messages on the form, and position the cursor on the form. Each form statement below will be followed with an example of the form statements in 4GL code.

SET_FORMS FRS

When the user moves out of a field on the form, some type of action may need to be taken by the program. This action may include checking the data for valid values, determining if any fields have been left blank, or selecting data from the database. Additionally action may need to occur when the user selects a menu item. The set_forms frs **(Forms Run-Time System)** statement is used to establish when these activations should occur. The activation value of 1 turns the activation on, while 0 turns the activation off. In the example below the code sets activation to occur when the user moves backward out of a field and when a menu item is selected. Moving forward out of a field (nextfield) has the default of 1 and does not need to be specified.

> **set_forms frs (activate (previousfield = 1,**
> **activate (menu) = 1);**

INITTABLE

The display mode of a table field on a form can be set to reflect the purpose of the table field. Mode types for table fields are read (view only), update (update and delete only), or fill (update, delete, and insert rows). The code below sets the table field mode to "fill" so that inventory items may be updated, deleted, or inserted into the INVENTORY table.

inittable inventorytbl fill;

INQUIRE_FORMS

Inquire_forms statements are used to retrieve information about the form or fields on the form. In the following example the INGRES constant rowno is retrieved into the field Row_no. This field is an integer value and will contain the table field row of the cursor position on the form. The empty string, indicated by ", means default to the table field name that is on the form.

inquire_forms table " (row_no = rowno);

The next inquire_forms statement retrieves the INGRES constant change into the field Anychange. Anychange is an integer value indicating whether the form has had changes made since the data was initially displayed on the form. Anychange is set to 1 if the form has changed, and to 0 if the form has not changed.

inquire_forms form (anychange = change);

INSERTROW

Insertrow inserts a new row in a table field on a form. The example code below is used when a new row needs to be inserted into the table field. First the inquire_forms statement determines what is the current table field row. Then 1 is subtracted from the row_no. This will permit the new row to be inserted at the current cursor position. Then the insertrow statement specifies the table field name and inserts the row into the table field.

inquire_forms table " (row_no = rowno);
row_no = row_no − 1;
insertrow inventorytbl[:row_no];

DELETEROW

Deleterow deletes a row from a table field on a form. The example code is used to delete a row from a table field named Inventorytbl. A row from the table field on the form will be deleted at the current cursor position.

deleterow inventorytbl;

In Figure 9.3 salesperson 1003 is displayed.

```
              MAINTAIN SALES STAFF INFORMATION

           Arizona Widget Wholesale Supply Company

    ┌────────┬─────────────────┬─────────────────┬─────────────────┐
    │ Number │    Last Name    │   First Name    │    Location     │
    ├────────┼─────────────────┼─────────────────┼─────────────────┤
    │ 1001   │ Barton          │ Jane            │ Phoenix         │
    │ 1002   │ Castro          │ Robert          │ Phoenix         │
    │ 1003   │ Barton          │ Jane            │ Phoenix         │
    │ 2001   │ Smith           │ John            │ Las Vegas       │
    │ 3001   │ Santos          │ Clarissa        │ San Diego       │
    │ 4001   │ Travis          │ Randy           │ El Paso         │
    │        │                 │                 │                 │
    │        │                 │                 │                 │
    │        │                 │                 │                 │
    │        │                 │                 │                 │
    └────────┴─────────────────┴─────────────────┴─────────────────┘

  Save      Delete      Insert      Exit(PF3)
```

FIGURE 9.3 *Maintain Sales Staff Information*

When Delete(2) is selected from the menu options, this row is deleted from the form as shown in Figure 9.4.

```
              MAINTAIN SALES STAFF INFORMATION

           Arizona Widget Wholesale Supply Company

    ┌────────┬─────────────────┬─────────────────┬─────────────────┐
    │ Number │    Last Name    │   First Name    │    Location     │
    ├────────┼─────────────────┼─────────────────┼─────────────────┤
    │ 1001   │ Barton          │ Jane            │ Phoenix         │
    │ 1002   │ Castro          │ Robert          │ Phoenix         │
    │ 2001   │ Smith           │ John            │ Las Vegas       │
    │ 3001   │ Santos          │ Clarissa        │ San Diego       │
    │ 4001   │ Travis          │ Randy           │ El Paso         │
    │        │                 │                 │                 │
    │        │                 │                 │                 │
    │        │                 │                 │                 │
    │        │                 │                 │                 │
    └────────┴─────────────────┴─────────────────┴─────────────────┘

  Save      Delete      Insert      Exit(PF3)
```

FIGURE 9.4 *Row Deleted*

UNLOADTABLE

The unloadtable statement unloads one row at a time from a table field for processing. Any statements within the begin and end block will execute once for each row in the table field. In the example below a table field is unloaded to delete rows from the table INVENTORY. The statement specifies that the table field named Inventorytbl is to be processed one row at a time. The INGRES variable state is retrieved into the field state. The field is an integer that will contain a value indicating if the row has been appended, unchanged, modified, or deleted from the table field Inventorytbl. A value of 4 indicates this row has been deleted from the table field on the form and should be deleted from the database. (Remember, deleterow deletes a row from a form, not from the database.)

```
unloadtable inventorytbl (state = _state)
begin
    if (state = 4) then
    delete from inventory
    where partno = :inventorytbl.partno;
end
```

RESUME

This statement stops the current processing and positions the cursor on the form. The cursor may be placed on a particular field or on the menu. The following statement stops the current processing and positions the cursor on the next field on the form.

```
resume next;
```

When a quantity is entered for an order, the price will be automatically calculated and displayed on the form. After the price is determined, the resume next command will move the cursor to the next available input column, Salespeople.

```
                    MAINTAIN CUSTOMER ORDERS
                Arizona Widget Wholesale Supply Company

Customer Number: 8113       Customer Name: Arizona Supply
        Address: 65 S. Central
           City: Phoenix
          State: AZ              Zip: 85012
          Phone: 602-271-4955
```

Salespeople	Part	Order Date	Delivery Date	Qty	Price
1001	9114	2/18/89	2/28/89	1	$ 36.99
1002	**9113**	**1/30/89**	**2/28/89**	**10**	**$ 13.00**

```
Save      Delete      Insert      Find      Blank      Exit(PF3)
```

FIGURE 9.5 *Cursor Moved to Next Input Column*

The next example stops the current processing, but positions the cursor on a specific field on the form, Customer Number (cusno).

resume field cusno;

```
                    MAINTAIN CUSTOMER ORDERS
                Arizona Widget Wholesale Supply Company

Customer Number: 1234       Customer Name:
        Address:
           City:
          State:                 Zip:
          Phone:
```

Salespeople	Part	Order Date	Delivery Date	Qty	Price
—					

```
Save      Delete      Insert      Find      Blank      Exit(PF3)
```

FIGURE 9.6 *Cursor Positioned on Specific Field*

When a customer number is not found in the database, resume field cusno positions the cursor on the field Customer Number on the form as was shown in Figure 9.6.

MESSAGE

The message statement displays a string on a form and is used to display a message to the user.

The following statement causes a message to be displayed when a user attempts to add to the database a customer that already exists in the database.

message 'Problem adding customer . . .';

```
                    MAINTAIN CUSTOMER INFORMATION
                 Arizona Widget Wholesale Supply Company

 Customer Number: 8113

   Customer Name: Arizona Supply

         Address: 65 S. Central

            City: Phoenix

           State: AZ             Zip: 85012

           Phone: 602-271-4955




 Problem adding customer ...    [ ]
```

FIGURE 9.7 *Message Displayed with Message Statement*

SLEEP

The sleep statement stops processing for a specified number of seconds. In this example the message will be displayed on the form for two seconds.

message 'Customer not found . . .';
sleep 2;

PROMPT

Prompt is used to accept input from the user. The prompt message will be displayed on the form and will then wait for the user's input. In this example the prompt message will appear on the menu line and the user's response will be accepted into the field called Answer.

answer =
    prompt 'Are you sure you want to delete this customer? (y/n)'
     with style = menuline;

```
                    MAINTAIN CUSTOMER INFORMATION
                Arizona Widget Wholesale Supply Company

Customer Number: 8113

  Customer Name: Arizona Supply

        Address: 65 S. Central

           City: Phoenix

          State: AZ              Zip: 85012

          Phone: 602-271-4955




Are you sure you want to delete this customer (Y/N)?  ☐
```

FIGURE 9.8 *Prompt for Input*

CLEAR FIELD

This statement is used to clear fields on a form. In this example all fields on the Customer form will be blanked out.

    clear field all;

Selecting Blank(5) from the menu options will activate the code that will result in clearing all values from the form, as shown in Figures 9.9 and 9.10.

```
                    MAINTAIN CUSTOMER INFORMATION
                Arizona Widget Wholesale Supply Company

 Customer Number: [8113 ]

   Customer Name: Arizona Supply

         Address: 65 S. Central

            City: Phoenix

           State: AZ              Zip: 85012

           Phone: 602-271-4955



 Add     Update     Delete     Find     Blank     Exit(PF3)
```

FIGURE 9.9 *Customer Information*

```
                    MAINTAIN CUSTOMER INFORMATION
                Arizona Widget Wholesale Supply Company

 Customer Number: [ ]

   Customer Name:

         Address:

            City:

           State:                 Zip:

           Phone:



 Add     Update     Delete     Find     Blank     Exit(PF3)
```

FIGURE 9.10 *All Fields Cleared with Blank Option*

DATABASE STATEMENTS

While forms statements act upon forms, database statements act upon the database and table rows in the database. They are used to retrieve, insert, update, and delete data from a database. Many of these database statements used in INGRES applications will be the same as the database statements mentioned in Chapters 4 and 5. However, these statements are part of the INGRES 4GL.

SELECT

The SELECT statement retrieves rows into a form object. Rows can be retrieved into a form name (one row on the form) or a table field name (multiple rows on the form). The example code below selects a row from the CUSTOMER table into the form name. The * is a wildcard that means select all columns from the CUSTOMER table. The : indicates this is a field from the form. The WHERE clause will retrieve the customer information from the CUSTOMER table where custno is equal to the customer number (:cusno) the user has entered on the form.

> **customer = select ***
> **from customer**
> **where custno = :cusno;**

This form uses the SELECT statement to put a single row on the form.

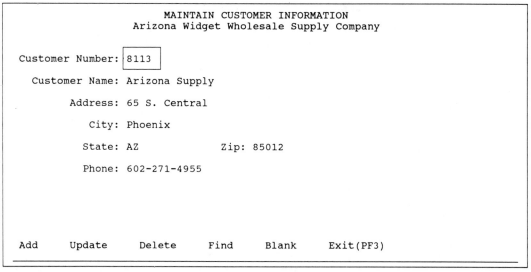

```
                    MAINTAIN CUSTOMER INFORMATION
                  Arizona Widget Wholesale Supply Company

  Customer Number: 8113

    Customer Name: Arizona Supply

          Address: 65 S. Central

             City: Phoenix

            State: AZ            Zip: 85012

            Phone: 602-271-4955



  Add      Update     Delete     Find     Blank     Exit(PF3)
```

FIGURE 9.11   *Selected Customer Information*

The code below selects multiple rows from the INVENTORY table into the table field Inventorytbl. Notice there is no WHERE clause, so all rows will be retrieved.

> **inventorytbl = select partno,**
> **qty,**
> **itemname,**
> **reorder,**
> **cost,**
> **price**
> **from inventory;**

The table field on this form uses the SELECT statement to retrieve one or more rows.

```
┌─────────────────────────────────────────────────────────────────────────┐
│                   MAINTAIN INVENTORY INFORMATION                          │
│                                                                           │
│             Arizona Widget Wholesale Supply Company                       │
│                                                                           │
│  ┌────────┬─────┬────────────────────────┬────────┬───────┬───────┐       │
│  │ Number │ Qty │      Description        │ Reorder│ Cost  │ Price │       │
│  ├────────┼─────┼────────────────────────┼────────┼───────┼───────┤       │
│  │ 9111   │2000 │ wrench                  │  100   │$ 1.35 │$ 1.95 │       │
│  │ 9112   │ 100 │ socket set              │   20   │$14.95 │$21.70 │       │
│  │ 9113   │ 250 │ scrwdrvr,#2             │   50   │$  .89 │$ 1.30 │       │
│  │ 9114   │  60 │ test meter, M5          │   10   │$25.50 │$36.99 │       │
│  │ 9115   │3500 │ pliers, 3 inch          │  200   │$ 1.50 │$ 2.18 │       │
│  │        │     │                         │        │       │       │       │
│  │        │     │                         │        │       │       │       │
│  │        │     │                         │        │       │       │       │
│  └────────┴─────┴────────────────────────┴────────┴───────┴───────┘       │
│                                                                           │
│   Save      Delete      Insert      Exit(PF3)                             │
└─────────────────────────────────────────────────────────────────────────┘
```

FIGURE 9.12   *Selected Inventory Information*

INSERT

This statement inserts a row into the database table. The following code will insert all the columns in the CUSTOMER table using the fields on the form. The values clause indicates that the form named customer will contain all the columns in the CUSTOMER table. After the user has entered the data on the form, this statement inserts a row:

```
insert into customer(*)
values (customer.all);
```

```
                MAINTAIN CUSTOMER INFORMATION
              Arizona Widget Wholesale Supply Company

  Customer Number: ┌──────┐
                   │ 1234 │
                   └──────┘
    Customer Name: New Customer

          Address: Any Address

             City: Any City

            State: AZ              Zip: 85000

            Phone: 602 111-1111




  Add     Update     Delete     Find     Blank     Exit(PF3)
```

FIGURE 9.13 *Maintain Customer Information*

The next statement inserts a row into the INVENTORY table, but the values clause uses a row from a table field on the form.

insert into inventory (partno, qty, itemname, reorder, cost, price)
values (:inventorytbl.partno,   :inventorytbl.qty,
        :inventorytbl.itemname, :inventorytbl.reorder,
        :inventorytbl.cost,   :inventorytbl.price);

UPDATE

This statement updates a row in the database table. The following code will update a row in the CUSTOMER table using values from the form.

update customer
set cusname   = :cusname,
    cusaddress = :cusaddress,
    cuscity   = :cuscity,
    cusstate   = :cusstate,
    cuszip   = :cuszip,
    cusphone   = :cusphone
where cusno   = :cusno;

```
                    MAINTAIN CUSTOMER INFORMATION
                 Arizona Widget Wholesale Supply Company

    Customer Number: 8111

      Customer Name: Atlas Supply

            Address: New Address      □

               City: Phoenix

              State: AZ              Zip: 85012

              Phone: 602 111-1111




    Add      Update      Delete      Find      Blank      Exit(PF3)
```

FIGURE 9.14 *Maintain Customer Information*

After the user has changed data on the form, this statement updates a row in the INVENTORY table, but the values clause uses a row from a table field on the form.

```
update inventory
set partno      = :inventorytbl.partno,
    qty         = :inventorytbl.qty,
    itemname    = :inventorytbl.itemname,
    reorder     = :inventorytbl.reorder,
    cost        = :inventory.cost,
    price       = :inventory.price
where partno    = :inventory.old_partno;
```

DELETE

The DELETE statement removes a row from the database table. The WHERE clause uses the value of cusno from the form.

```
delete from customer
where cusno = :cusno;
```

The next statement deletes a row from the database table, but the WHERE clause uses the value of the table field column from the form.

```
delete from inventory
where partno = :inventory.partno;
```

INQUIRE_INGRES

The INQUIRE_INGRES statement retrieves INGRES constants that indicate the result of a database access. The constant rowno is retrieved into the integer field named row_count to determine if a row was retrieved from a table. The constant errorno is retrieved into the integer field named error_no. The value of 0 indicates no error has occurred.

```
customer = select *
from customer
where cusno = :cusno;

inquire_ingres (row_count = rowcount,
                error_no = errorno);
```

When this customer information is selected from the database, the INGRES constant rowcount will contain the value 1 indicating a row was retrieved from the database, and the constant errorno will contain the value 0 indicating no errors have occurred.

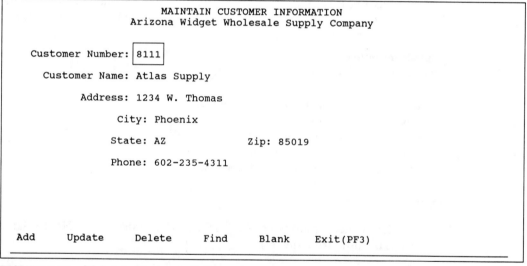

FIGURE 9.15 *Maintain Customer Information*

When a customer number is not found in the database, the INGRES constant rowcount will contain the value 0, and the constant errorno will contain the value 0.

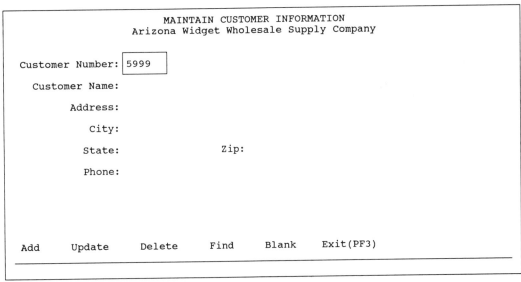

```
                    MAINTAIN CUSTOMER INFORMATION
                 Arizona Widget Wholesale Supply Company

  Customer Number: │5999  │

    Customer Name:

          Address:

             City:

            State:                    Zip:

            Phone:




  Add     Update     Delete     Find     Blank     Exit(PF3)
```

FIGURE 9.16   *Customer 5999 Not Found in Database*

ACTIVATION STATEMENTS

In 4GL programs the statements are organized into activation blocks. There are four activation types: initialize, menu, field, and key. Any 4GL code within the block will be executed depending on the type of activation.

INITIALIZE

The initialize section is the activation block that is always the first section of a 4GL program. This is where fields (variables) needed for processing are declared and initialized. Variables declared in the initialize block are known as "hidden" fields and columns. These fields do not exist on the form. In the following example three fields are declared in the initialize section.

```
initialize (
      answer     = char(1)        not null with default,
      error_no   = integer2       not null with default,
      row_count  = integer2       not null with default) =
begin
end
```

In the next example hidden fields and a column are declared. The hidden column is a column of the table field on the form, but is not displayed. Between the begin and end markers the table field is initialized to fill (insert, update, delete are possible) and the INVENTORY table is retrieved into the table field Inventorytbl. Because the

Figure 9.20 shows the form after the menu activation of Blank(5).

```
                      MAINTAIN CUSTOMER INFORMATION
                   Arizona Widget Wholesale Supply Company

  Customer Number:  [ ]

    Customer Name:

          Address:

             City:

            State:              Zip:

            Phone:




  Add      Update      Delete      Find      Blank      Exit(PF3)
```

FIGURE 9.20 *Form After Activation of Blank*

FIELD

Field activation is executed when a user moves out of a field. In the following example the 4GL code that is within the begin and end markers is executed whenever the user moves out of the field Cusno. The value the user has entered on the form will be used to retrieve a row from the CUSTOMER table as shown in Figure 9.21.

```
field 'cusno' =
begin

    customer = select *
    from customer
    where cusno = :cusno;

  inquire_ingres (row_count = rowcount,
                  error_no = errorno);

    if (row_count = 0 or error_no != 0) then
        message 'Customer not found ...';
        sleep 2;
        clear field cusname, cusaddress, cuscity,
                    cusstate, cuszip, cusphone;
    endif;
    resume;
end
```

FIGURE 9.21 *Field Activation*

When a customer number is entered on the form, field activation will be executed and the cursor will move to the next field on the form as in Figure 9.22.

```
┌─────────────────────────────────────────────────────────────────────────┐
│                     MAINTAIN CUSTOMER INFORMATION                         │
│                 Arizona Widget Wholesale Supply Company                   │
│                                                                           │
│   Customer Number: 1234                                                   │
│                     ┌─┐                                                    │
│     Customer Name:  └─┘                                                    │
│                                                                           │
│          Address:                                                         │
│                                                                           │
│             City:                                                         │
│                                                                           │
│            State:                    Zip:                                 │
│                                                                           │
│            Phone:                                                         │
│                                                                           │
│                                                                           │
│                                                                           │
│   Add     Update     Delete     Find     Blank     Exit(PF3)              │
│                                                                           │
└─────────────────────────────────────────────────────────────────────────┘
```

FIGURE 9.22 *Field Activation Executed*

Since customer number 1234 was not found in the database, the field activation displays a message on the form in Figure 9.23.

```
┌─────────────────────────────────────────────────────────────────────────┐
│                     MAINTAIN CUSTOMER INFORMATION                         │
│                 Arizona Widget Wholesale Supply Company                   │
│                                                                           │
│   Customer Number: 1234                                                   │
│                                                                           │
│     Customer Name:                                                        │
│                                                                           │
│          Address:                                                         │
│                                                                           │
│             City:                                                         │
│                                                                           │
│            State:                    Zip:                                 │
│                                                                           │
│            Phone:                                                         │
│                                                                           │
│                                                                           │
│                                  ┌─┐                                       │
│   Customer not found ...         └─┘                                       │
│                                                                           │
└─────────────────────────────────────────────────────────────────────────┘
```

FIGURE 9.23 *Field Activation Displays Message*

KEY

Key activation is used to assign a specific key on the keyboard to a block of code. Using key activation, an application can consistently associate a menu option with one key. In this example key equated to frskey3 will always be used for the menu option 'Exit'.

```
'Exit', key frskey3 =
begin
/*
      Return to topframe.
*/
      return;
end
```

```
              MAINTAIN INVENTORY INFORMATION

           Arizona Widget Wholesale Supply Company


 Number  Qty              Description          Reorder   Cost    Price

 9111   2000  wrench                            100    $ 1.35  $ 1.95
 9112    100  socket set                         20    $14.95  $21.70
 9113    250  scrwdrvr,#2                         50    $  .89  $ 1.30
 9114     60  test meter, M5                      10    $25.50  $36.99
 9115   3500  pliers, 3 inch                     200    $ 1.50  $ 2.18




 Save      Delete      Insert      Exit(PF3)
```

FIGURE 9.24 *Key Activation for Exit*

▆ COMMUNICATION BETWEEN FRAMES

RETURN

The return statement returns the user to the previous frame. In the example below the return statement returns the user to the calling frame, topframe.

```
'Exit', key frskey3 =
begin
/*
```

Return to topframe.
```
*/
    return;
end
```

EXIT

The exit statement completely exits the application. In the following example the exit statement quits the application and returns control to where the application started.

```
'Exit', key frskey3 =
begin
/*
    Exit the application
*/
    exit;
end
```

CALLFRAME

The statement callframe transfers control from one frame to another. In this example the menu item 'Customer' in topframe will call the frame customer. The empty parentheses, ( ), indicate no values are passed to the frame customer.

```
'Customer' =
begin
    callframe customer( );
end
```

In the example below the menu item 'Find' in the customer frame calls the frame named popcusname and passes the field Cusno by reference. When a field is passed by reference, the value of cusno selected in the frame popcusname will be reflected in the contents of the field Cusno in the customer frame.

```
'Find' =
    begin
    /*
        Provide help window
    */
        callframe popcusname (cusno = byref(:cusno));
    end
```

Select menu option Find(4).

```
                    MAINTAIN CUSTOMER INFORMATION
                 Arizona Widget Wholesale Supply Company

  Customer Number: ▢

    Customer Name:

          Address:

             City:

            State:              Zip:

            Phone:




  Add      Update     Delete     Find      Blank     Exit(PF3)
```

FIGURE 9.25   *Using Find Option*

The help popup window is called and displayed.

```
                    MAINTAIN CUSTOMER INFORMATION
                 Arizona Widget Wholesale Supply Company


  Customer Number: 0

  Cu ┌────────┬───────────────────┬──────────────────┬───────────────┐
     │ Number │   Customer Name   │     Address      │     Phone     │
     ├────────┼───────────────────┼──────────────────┼───────────────┤
     │  8113  │ Arizona Supply    │ 65 S. Central    │ 602-271-4955  │
     │  8111  │ Atlas Supply      │ 1234 W. Thomas   │ 602-235-4311  │
     │  8114  │ Desert Vendors    │ 33 N. Outerloop  │ 215-333-4111  │
     │  8116  │ Ocean Supply      │ 65 Marine Way    │ 591-695-2211  │
     │  8112  │ Saguaro Wholesale │ 351 Highland     │ 602-344-6000  │
     │  8115  │ Western Wholesale │ 2501 Lee Trevino │ 415-222-6111  │
     │        │                   │                  │               │
     └────────┴───────────────────┴──────────────────┴───────────────┘


  Select          Exit(PF3)
```

FIGURE 9.26   *Help Popup Window Displayed*

Chapter 10

CREATING AN INGRES APPLICATION

CREATING AN APPLICATION

You will use the database and tables created in Chapter 2 for your application. If you have not already done so, refer to Chapter 2 to create your tables. When the database and tables have been created, you can create an application.

Now that we have introduced ABF components (frames, forms, and code), form statements, database statements, activation statements, and communication between frames, we are ready to create an application. ABF is accessed at the operating system prompt by typing **abf** <**databasename**>, where <database name> refers to the database you wish to use for your application. For our application the database name is "Order" and the application name will be "Sample." To start ABF enter the following command.

abf order

Press **Return**, and the Applications Catalog screen will appear as shown in Figure 10.1. This screen lists all applications that belong to this database.

```
ABF - Applications Catalog

Name                    Owner    Short Remark




Place cursor on row and select desired operation from menu.

Create      Destroy      Edit      Rename      MoreInfo      >
```

FIGURE 10.1 *Applications Catalog Screen*

The Applications Catalog menu options are as follows:

Create	Begins creation of a new application.
Destroy	Destroys the selected application.
Edit	Edits the selected application.
Rename	Renames the selected application.
MoreInfo	Displays more information about the selected application.
Go	Runs the application for testing, whether it is complete or incomplete.
Utilities	Brings up the Utilities menu.
Find	Finds a specified string in the application list.
Top	Scrolls to the top of the application list.
Bottom	Scrolls to the bottom of the application list.
Help	Displays onscreen information about this frame.
Quit	Exits ABF.

Select **Create** from the menu and you will see the screen in Figure 10.2. Enter **sample** for the application name and a short remark about the application. Next select the application language. This may be SQL or QUEL. The language that appears on this screen is the default language for the application. The application examples in this chapter will use SQL only. "Source Directory" is the directory location for your 4GL code. "Long Remark" is used for documentation; in this instance it just explains the components of this application.

```
ABF - Create an Application


  Name: sample                  Created: 17-feb-1990 10:28:11

 Owner: Username              Modified:

 Short Remark: Sample Application for Order Database

 Language:  SQL    Source Directory:
                   SIS1:[USERNAME.INGRES.ORDER]


 Long Remark:
 ┌─────────────────────────────────────────────────────────┐
 │ Sample is an example order entry system consisting of a  │
 │ topframe, four, frames, and one popup help window.       │
 │                                                          │
 │                                                          │
 │                                                          │
 │                                                          │
 │                                                          │
 └─────────────────────────────────────────────────────────┘

 Create    Forget    Help
```

FIGURE 10.2 *Create an Application Screen*

The Create an Application menu options are as follows:

Create   Begins creation of a new application.

Forget   Cancels the create operation and returns to previous frame.

Help   Displays Help frame.

EDITING AN APPLICATION

Once the application has been created, select **Edit**. You should now see the Edit an Application screen (Figure 10.3). (The next time you want to work with the application called sample, just type in **abf order sample** to go directly to ABF Edit an Application.)

```
ABF - Edit an Application

 Name: sample                              Default Start:
                                           Query Language: SQL

┌──────────────────────────┬──────────┬─────────────────────────┐
│ Frame/Procedure Name      │ Type     │ Short Remark            │
│                           │          │                         │
├──────────────────────────┼──────────┼─────────────────────────┤
│                           │          │                         │
│                           │          │                         │
│                           │          │                         │
│                           │          │                         │
│                           │          │                         │
│                           │          │                         │
│                           │          │                         │
└──────────────────────────┴──────────┴─────────────────────────┘

 Place cursor on row and select desired operation from menu.

 Create     Destroy     Edit     Rename      MoreInfo
```

FIGURE 10.3 *Edit an Application Screen*

The Edit an Application menu options are as follows:

Create	Begins creation of a new frame or procedure.
Destroy	Destroys the selected frame or procedure definition and removes it from the application.
Edit	Edits the selected frame or procedure.
Rename	Renames the selected frame or procedure.
MoreInfo	Displays more information about the selected frame or procedure.
Defaults	Displays application-specific defaults.
Utilities	Brings up the Utilities menu.
Find	Finds a specified string in the frame/procedure list.
End	Standard operation to leave INGRES.

■■■ CREATING A FRAME

Now that the application has been created, you will create the application's frames. First you will create the menu frame for the application. This frame will be called "topframe." To create this frame select **Create** from the Edit an Application menu. The popup window, Create a Frame or Procedure, will appear (Figure 10.4). (Remember, the frame is the object that associates a form with source code.)

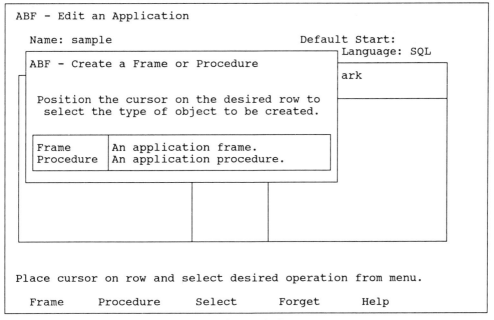

FIGURE 10.4 *Create a Frame or Procedure Window*

The menu options for Create a Frame or Procedure are as follows:

Frame	Selects Frame as type of object to be created.
Procedure	Selects Procedure as the type of object to be created.
Select	Selects the current row as the type of object to be created.
Forget	Cancels the create operation and returns to the previous frame.

Select **Frame** from the menu. Next we will choose the frame type. As shown in Figure 10.5, frames can be user specified, an INGRES report, or Query-By-Forms. The menu frame we are creating is user specified since we will create a form and write source code for this frame. So select **USER** from the list of frame types.

Create the form by selecting **FormEdit** from the menu. Notice the form name defaults to the same as the frame name. Also, the source code will default to the frame name with the file extension of .osq. This file extension indicates the source code is INGRES 4GL. You will get a message that the form topframe was not found. Press **Return**, and the VIFRED Forms Catalog will be displayed (Figure 10.8). The VIFRED Forms Catalog menu options are:

Create	Displays a menu of operations for creating a new form.
Destroy	Destroys the form highlighted by the cursor. You may only destroy forms that you own.
Edit	Displays the Form Layout frame for editing or viewing the form selected.
Rename	Renames the form selected. You may only rename forms that you own.
MoreInfo	Obtains more information about the selected form. The additional information includes the time the form was created and a short and long description of the form.
Utilities	Brings up the Utilities menu.

```
VIFRED - Forms Catalog

 ┌─────────────────────────┬──────────────┬─────────────────────┐
 │ Name                    │ Owner        │ Short Remark        │
 ├─────────────────────────┼──────────────┼─────────────────────┤
 │                         │              │                     │
 │                         │              │                     │
 │                         │              │                     │
 │                         │              │                     │
 │                         │              │                     │
 │                         │              │                     │
 │                         │              │                     │
 │                         │              │                     │
 └─────────────────────────┴──────────────┴─────────────────────┘

    Place cursor on row and select desired operation from menu.

     Create      Destroy      Edit      Rename      MoreInfo
```

FIGURE 10.8 *VIFRED Menu*

Select **Create** from the menu to create the form for topframe. Once a form has been created for an application, always edit the form from VIFRED within ABF. If you use the INGRES subsystem VIFRED outside of ABF, any changes you make to a form will not show up in your application.

After you select Create a submenu will appear (Figure 10.9). The VIFRED Create Form menu options are as follows:

BlankForm	Displays a blank screen on which you can create a new form.
TableDefault	Prompts for table name and creates default form for the table.
JoinDefDefault	Displays a default layout for a JoinDef that you can edit.

Select **BlankForm** to create the form for topframe. The form as it will appear when completed is shown in Figure 10.10. Use the VIFRED menu options discussed in Chapter 3 to create the form. Remember to save your form and enter a short comment to indicate the purpose of the form. You can find more detailed information about this form in Appendix C.

```
VIFRED - Forms Catalog

 ┌───────────────────────────┬──────────┬──────────────────────┐
 │ Name                      │ Owner    │ Short Remark         │
 ├───────────────────────────┼──────────┼──────────────────────┤
 │                           │          │                      │
 │                           │          │                      │
 │                           │          │                      │
 │                           │          │                      │
 │                           │          │                      │
 │                           │          │                      │
 │                           │          │                      │
 └───────────────────────────┴──────────┴──────────────────────┘

 Place cursor on row and select desired operation from menu.

   BlankForm     TableDefault     JoinDefDefault     Help
```

FIGURE 10.9   *VIFRED Create Form Menu*

```
        ARIZONA WIDGET WHOLESALE SUPPLY COMPANY
                234 N. CENTRAL AVENUE
                PHOENIX, ARIZONA 85001
                   602-251-6000

        +--------------------------------------------+
        |                                            |
        |                 Main Menu                  |
        |                                            |
        |    (1)   Enter customer orders             |
        |    (2)   Maintain customer information      |
        |    (3)   Maintain inventory                |
        |    (4)   Maintain sales staff information  |
        |                                            |
        |                                            |
        +--------------------------------------------+

     ------------------------End-of-Form------------------------
```

FIGURE 10.10   *Topframe Main Menu*

CREATING SOURCE CODE

Now that we have created a frame and the associated form, we need to write the source code for this frame. This frame will use INGRES menu activation. By using menu activation the menu items will appear on the menu line. When the application is run, any code within the menu block will be executed.

The topframe menu options are as follows:

Menu Option	Function	Called Frame
OrderEntry	Enter customer orders	orderentry
Customer	Maintain customer information	customer
Inventory	Maintain inventory	inventory
Salespeople	Maintain staff information	salespeople

Figure 10.11 shows the code for the topframe. The initialize section must always appear first in a 4GL program. It is used to declare variables and assign initial values. The initialize section executes only once for each time a frame is called.

From the ABF - Edit a USER Frame Definition screen (Figure 10.7), select **Edit.** When you select Edit INGRES starts up the text editor. Use the editor to enter the 4GL source code in Figure 10.11. Note that INGRES 4GL comments are delimited by /* at the beginning of a comment and */ at the end of a comment.

```
/*
   Frame:      Main Menu for application Sample (topframe.osq)
   Author:     Your_Name
   Purpose:    To allow the user to select the desired option
               from the main menu.
*/

initialize () =
begin

/*
    Set autocommit on.  If you prefer, you may set autocommit off
    and use commit after each database statement.
*/
    commit;
    set autocommit on;
/*
    Set field activation to occur whenever the user moves
    backward out of a field or selects a menu key.  The default
    is already set for field activation to occur whenever the
    user moves forward out of a field.
*/

    set_forms frs (activate (previousfield) = 1,
                   activate (menu) = 1);

end

'OrderEntry' =
begin

    callframe orderentry();
end

'Customer' =
begin

    callframe customer();
end

'Inventory' =
begin

    callframe inventory();
end

'Salespeople' =
begin

    callframe salespeople();
end

'Exit', key frskey3 =
begin

/*
    Exit the application.
*/

    exit;
end
```

FIGURE 10.11 *Topframe.osq*

COMPILING A FRAME

After you have entered the source code for the topframe and saved the code, you can compile this frame. Select **Compile** from the ABF - Edit a USER Frame Definition screen (Figure 10.7). If any errors are found messages will be displayed on the screen. When topframe compiles without any errors, select **Go** from the menu to test this frame. When you test the frame you should see the form you created with the menu options from the 4GL program.

◼ CREATING A FRAME WITH SIMPLE FIELDS

Next you will create the frame to maintain customer information for the CUSTO-MER table. The form will display just one customer at a time. Create the frame "customer" just like you created topframe. Then select **FormEdit** from the ABF - Edit a USER Frame Definition screen (Figure 10.7) and then **Create** (Figure 10.8). This time instead of selecting BlankForm choose **TableDefault** (Figure 10.9). You will be prompted for a table name. Enter the table name **customer**.

```
VIFRED - Forms Catalog

 ┌────────────────────────┬─────────┬──────────────────────────┐
 │ Name                   │ Owner   │ Short Remark             │
 ├────────────────────────┼─────────┼──────────────────────────┤
 │ topframe               │ Username│ Main menu from sample Appl.│
 │                        │         │                          │
 │                        │         │                          │
 │                        │         │                          │
 │                        │         │                          │
 │                        │         │                          │
 │                        │         │                          │
 │                        │         │                          │
 └────────────────────────┴─────────┴──────────────────────────┘

  Place cursor on row and select desired operation from menu.

    SimpleFields      TableField      Help       End
```

FIGURE 10.12 *VIFRED TableDefault Menu*

As shown in Figure 10.12, the VIFRED TableDefault menu options are:

SimpleFields   Displays one record at a time.

TableField   Displays several rows on a form. These can be scrolled horizontally if all columns do not fit on the screen, and vertically if all rows do not fit on the frame.

Select **SimpleFields**. Edit the default screen for the CUSTOMER table to look like Figure 10.13. Define the field attributes as Reverse Video. A more detailed description of the form and its fields can be found in Appendix C.

```
                   MAINTAIN CUSTOMER INFORMATION
                Arizona Widget Wholesale Supply Company


Customer Number: i___

  Customer Name: c_____

        Address: c_____

           City: c_____

          State: c_            Zip: c____

          Phone: c_____

-------------------End-of-Form----------------------
```

FIGURE 10.13   *Maintain Customer Form*

MENU ACTIVATION

The customer frame will use menu activation to call another frame to provide a popup help window listing all customers in the database. The frame popcusname will be called, and cusno will be passed by reference. This means that whatever customer is selected in the popup help window, that customer's cusno will be used to retrieve customer information in the frame customer. The code to call the popup help window looks like this:

```
'Find' =

begin

 /*
    Provide help window, then retrieve the customer
    information and place the cursor on the field
    customer name (cusname).
 */

    callframe popframe (cusno = byref(:cusno)):
    customer = select *
             from customer
             where cusno = :cusno;
    resume field cusname;
end
```

FIGURE 10.14   *Find Field*

FIELD ACTIVATION

Besides menu activation, the customer frame uses field activation. Each time the cursor moves forward or backward out of a field on the form, the block of code associated with the field in the 4GL code will be executed. The following example will retrieve a customer's information when the cursor moves out of the field Cusno. The select statement retrieves the Customer row from the table into the form called customer. The colon (:) before variables shows that the variable belongs to the form or has been declared in the initialize block. In other words, it is not a database column name.

field 'cusno' =
begin

/*
    If customer number has been entered on the screen, get the
    customer information and place cursor on next field on the form.
*/

    customer = select *
             from customer
             where cusno = :cusno;
    resume next;
end

KEY ACTIVATION

This program also uses key activation. INGRES will map a frskey (Forms Run-Time System) to a particular key. This helps keep applications consistent in the use of special keys. Using the same keys to perform the same function on all frames makes it easier for users to learn and use an application. This application uses the frskey3 to equate to the menu item 'Exit.' All frames in this application will use the same key to 'Exit.'

```
'Exit', key frskey3 =
begin

/*
    Return to topframe.
*/
    return;
end
```

The following 4GL is the code for customer.osq. Enter the 4GL code, compile, and test the program.

```
/*
    Frame:    Maintain Customer Information
    Purpose: To  add, change, or delete customers from the
             Order database.
*/
initialize (
    answer      = char(1)       not null with default,
    error_no    = integer2      not null with default,
    row_count   = integer2      not null with default) =
begin
end

field 'cusno' =
begin

/*
   If customer number has been entered on the screen, get the
   customer information.
*/
    customer = select *
    from customer
    where cusno = :cusno;

    inquire_ingres (row_count = rowcount,
                    error_no = errorno);

    if (row_count = 0 or error_no != 0) then
        message 'Customer not found ...';
        sleep 2;
        clear field cusname, cusaddress, cuscity, cusstate,
                    cuszip, cusphone;
    endif;

    resume next;
end

'Add' =
begin

/*
    Insert row.
*/
```

FIGURE 10.15   *Maintain Customer .osq*

```
            insert into customer (*)
            values (customer.all);
            inquire_ingres (row_count = rowcount,
                            error_no = errorno);

            if (row_count > 0 and error_no = 0) then
                message 'Customer added ...';
                sleep 2;

            elseif (row_count = 0 and error_no = 0) then
                message 'Customer was not added ...';
                sleep 2;

            elseif (error_no != 0) then
                message 'Problem adding customer ...';
                sleep 2;
            endif;

            resume field cusno;
        end

    'Update' =
    begin

    /*
        Update row.
    */

        update customer
        set cusname = :cusname,
            cusaddress = :cusaddress,
            cuscity = :cuscity,
            cusstate = :cusstate,
            cuszip = :cuszip,
            cusphone = :cusphone
        where cusno = :cusno;

        inquire_ingres (row_count = rowcount,
                        error_no = errorno);

        if (row_count > 0 and error_no = 0) then
            message 'Customer updated ...';
            sleep 2;

        elseif (row_count = 0 and error_no = 0) then
            message 'Customer was not updated ...';
            sleep 2;

        elseif (error_no != 0) then
            message 'Problem updating customer ...';
            sleep 2;
        endif;

        resume field cusno;
    end

    'Delete' =
    begin

    /*
        Verify the delete.
    */
```

FIGURE 10.15 *(Continued)*

```
        answer = prompt 'Are you sure you want to delete this
                        customer? (y/n)'
                with style = menuline;
        if (uppercase(answer) != 'Y') then
            resume field cusno;
        endif;

/*
    Delete row.
*/

        delete from customer
        where cusno = :cusno;

        inquire_ingres (row_count = rowcount,
                        error_no = errorno);

        if (row_count > 0 and error_no = 0) then
            message 'Customer deleted ...';
            sleep 2;
            clear field all;

        elseif (row_count = 0 and error_no = 0) then
            message 'Customer was not deleted ...';
            sleep 2;

        elseif (error_no != 0) then
            message 'Problem deleting customer ...';
            sleep 2;
        endif;

        inquire_ingres (row_count = rowcount,
                        error_no = errorno);

        resume field cusno;
    end

    'Find' =
    begin

/*
    Provide help window.
*/

        callframe popcusname (cusno = byref(:cusno));

        customer =   select *
                     from customer
                     where cusno = :cusno;

        resume field cusname;
    end

    'Blank' =

    begin

/*
    Blank all fields on the screen.
*/

        clear field all;
    end
```

FIGURE 10.15   *(Continued)*

```
'Exit', key frskey3 =
begin

/*
    Return to topframe.
*/
    return;
end
```

FIGURE 10.15 *(Continued)*

◼ CREATING A POPUP WINDOW

Next you will create the popup help window for the 'Find' menu activation in the frame called customer. When Find is selected from the menu, the block of code associated with this menu activation will call the frame popcusname. Create the frame just as you created the other frames. This time when you create the form you will select **TableDefault** and then choose **TableField** as the form default. Selecting Table-Field as the form default will display more than one row on the form at a time. Edit the form popcusname to look like Figure 10.16. A more detailed description of the form and its fields can be found in Appendix C.

Number	Customer Name	Address	Phone

```
           -- End-of-Form --
```

FIGURE 10.16 *Column Menu*

You will need to delete unwanted columns and set display attributes. After you have edited the form to look like Figure 10.16, you will specify that this is a popup window. Make sure you move the table field to the upper left corner of the form. Then select **FormAttr** from the menu. This will allow the frame to be defined as a popup frame (Figure 10.17). On the Form Attributes for popcusname type **popup** for the Style. The position will be "floating." This means the popup help window will position itself in coordination with the cursor position on the form. Since the table field already has a box around it, enter **n** for border. Now select **VisuallyAdjust** and then **Resize** and move the edges of the form up around the popup window. This completes the process of creating a popup window.

```
                Form Attributes for 'popcusname'

   Style (fullscreen/popup): popup          Size:    12 rows    73 cols

   Position (fixed/floating): floating      Border (y/n): n
```

FIGURE 10.17 *Attribute Menu*

The following is the 4GL code for popcusname.osq. Follow the same process as you did with the last two frames. Create the 4GL program, compile the frame, and test. When you test this frame start with the topframe, which will call the customer frame. When you get to the customer frame select the 'Find' menu option to test the popup window. Remember, there must be data in the CUSTOMER table for the popup window to display.

```
/*
    Frame:    Popup customer name selection (popcusname.osq)
    Purpose: To display a window of customer names.  The selected

             customer's customer number is passed back to the
             calling program.
*/
initialize
   (row_count           = integer2 not null with default,
    cusno                = integer2 not null with default,
    error_no             = integer2 not null with default) =

begin

    inittable customer read;
    customer = select cusno,
                      cusname,
                      cusaddress,
                      cusphone
               from customer
               order by cusname;

/*
    If no rows were found, give message and return to calling
    program.
*/
    inquire_ingres (row_count = rowcount,
                    error_no = errorno);

    if (row_count = 0 and error_no = 0) then
        message 'No rows found ...'
           with style = popup;
```

FIGURE 10.18 *Popcusname.osq*

```
            return;
        endif;
end

'Select', key frskey4 =
begin

/*
    Select desired customer and return customer number.
*/

    cusno = :customer.cusno;
    return;
end

'Exit', key frskey3 =
begin
    return;
end
```

FIGURE 10.18   *(Continued)*

▮▮▮ CREATING A FRAME WITH TABLE FIELDS

The last frame to be discussed in this chapter contains multiple rows on the form. The frame inventory will be used to enter inventory information. Create the form shown in Figure 10.19 using the INVENTORY table as the TableDefault. This will be the same process you used to create the popup frame. Use Appendix C to determine display attributes and number of rows to display on the form.

```
                    MAINTAIN INVENTORY INFORMATION
                  Arizona Widget Wholesale Supply Company

| Number | Qty |        Description        | Reorder | Cost | Price |
|--------|-----|---------------------------|---------|------|-------|
|        |     |                           |         |      |       |
|        |     |                           |         |      |       |
|        |     |                           |         |      |       |
|        |     |                           |         |      |       |
|        |     |                           |         |      |       |

                         -- End-of-Form --
```

FIGURE 10.19   *Inventory Frame*

Notice in Figure 10.19 the column "Number" on the form. Number is the column Partno from the INVENTORY table. When the table was created in Chapter 2

Partno was defined as the key to the INVENTORY table. Because Partno is a key field and can be changed on the form, when the rows from the INVENTORY table are selected into the form Partno will be saved in a hidden field column hold partno. Then if Partno changes on the form, the hidden field column will be used to update the row in the INVENTORY table since the hold partno will contain the key field value stored in the database.

Also, a hidden column called "status" will be used to determine if a row has been inserted into the table field on the form. Initially you will assign status the value of 2 for all rows selected from the INVENTORY table. When a new row is inserted into the table field, the new row's status will be set to 5.

INGRES also maintains a variable that checks to see whether a row in a table field has been appended to the bottom of the table field, changed since it was selected into the table field, or deleted from the table field. This variable is named "_state" and can be accessed during an unloadtable. Since _state does not identify when a row has been inserted within a table field (only appended), you will use the INGRES variable _state and the hidden column status to know when to insert or update a row.

The functions and values associated with _state and status are summarized below.

INGRES Unloadtable _state Values

Action	Description	_State
insert	Row appended to table field	1
select	Row loaded or inserted into table field	2
update	Row loaded or inserted into table field and modified	3
delete	Row loaded or inserted into table field and deleted	4

4GL Hidden Columns Values

Action	Description	Status
select	Row loaded into table field	2
insert	Row inserted by user into table field	5

When the user selects Save from the menu options, the table field will be unloaded and each row will be processed one at a time. The INGRES statement unloadtable is a control loop that unloads the table field one row at a time. You will use two unloadtable statements. The first unloadtable will delete rows from the database. The second unloadtable will insert and update rows in the database. Rows are deleted prior to inserts and updates since deleted rows are moved to the bottom of the data set by INGRES.

The following is the code for the frame inventory. Again, create the program, compile the program, and then test the program.

```
/*
    Frame:    Maintain inventory information (inventory.osq)
    Purpose: To add, insert, and delete inventory information.
*/

initialize (
    answer                     = char(1)  not null with default,
    anychange                  = integer2 not null with default,
    error_no                   = integer2 not null with default,
    inventorytbl.old_partno    = integer2 not null with default,
    inventorytbl.status        = integer2 not null with default,
    row_count                  = integer2 not null with default,
    row_no                     = integer2 not null with default,
    state                      = integer1 not null with default)=
begin

/*
    Initialize tablefield and select into tablefield.   Since
    partno is the key to this table, select partno into a hidden
    column so that if the partno on the screen changes, the
    update will use the hidden column in the where clause.  Also
    use the hidden column 'status' to determine when a row has
    been inserted into the tablefield.
*/

    inittable inventorytbl fill;

    inventorytbl =
        select  partno,
                qty,
                itemname,
                reorder,
                cost,
                price,
                status = 2,
                old_partno = partno
        from inventory;
end

'Save' =
begin

    message 'Saving ...';
/*
    Set autocommit off to do transactions in MTS mode.
*/
    set autocommit off;

/*
    Remove rows marked for delete first.
*/

    unloadtable inventorytbl (state = _state)
    begin
```

FIGURE 10.20 *Inventory.osq*

```
                    if (state = 4) then
                        delete from inventory
                        where partno = :inventorytbl.partno;

                        inquire_ingres (error_no = errorno);
                        if (error_no != 0) then
                            rollback;
                            commit;
                            set autocommit on;
                            message 'Problem updating rows ...';
                            sleep 2;
                            resume;
                        endif;
                    endif;
            end;

    /*
        Do insert and update to rows.
    */

        unloadtable inventorytbl (state = _state)
        begin
            if (state = 1 or inventorytbl.status = 5) then
                insert into inventory (partno,
                                       qty,
                                       itemname,
                                       reorder,
                                       cost,
                                       price)
                values (:inventorytbl.partno,
                        :inventorytbl.qty,
                        :inventorytbl.itemname,
                        :inventorytbl.reorder,
                        :inventorytbl.cost,
                        :inventorytbl.price);

            elseif (state = 3 and inventorytbl.status != 5) then
                update inventory
                set partno   = :inventorytbl.partno,
                    qty      = :inventorytbl.qty,
                    itemname = :inventorytbl.itemname,
                    reorder  = :inventorytbl.reorder,
                    cost     = :inventorytbl.cost,
                    price    = :inventorytbl.price
                where partno = :inventorytbl.old_partno;
            endif;

            inquire_ingres (error_no = errorno);
            if (error_no != 0) then
                rollback;
                commit;
                set autocommit on;
                message 'Problem updating rows ...';
                sleep 2;
```

FIGURE 10.20 *(Continued)*

```
                            resume;
                endif;
        end;

        commit;
        set autocommit on;

    /*
        Redisplay details.
    */

        inittable inventorytbl fill;

        inventorytbl =
            select  partno,
                    qty,
                    itemname,
                    reorder,
                    cost,
                    price,
                    status = 2,
                    old_partno = partno
            from inventory;
    /*
        Set the screen change flag to indicate changes have been
    saved.
    */

        set_forms form (change = 0);
        resume field inventorytbl;
    end

    'Delete' =
    begin

    /*
        Verify the delete.  If row is to be deleted from the
        tablefield, set the screen change flag.  The row will be
        deleted from the table  during the 'Save' processing.
    */

        answer = prompt 'Are you sure you want to delete this row?
                        (y/n)'
            with style = menuline;
        if (uppercase(answer) = 'Y') then
            deleterow inventorytbl;
            set_forms form (change = 1);
        endif;
    end

    'Insert' =
    begin

    /*
```

FIGURE 10.20   *(Continued)*

```
        Insert row into tablefield.  Set row status to '5' to
indicate this will be an insert.
*/

    inquire_forms table '' (row_no = rowno);
    row_no = row_no - 1;
    insertrow inventorytbl[:row_no];
    inventorytbl.status = 5;
end

'Exit', key frskey3 =
begin

/*
    Determine if a row(s) have been deleted from table, rows
updated, or rows added.  If change was found, make sure user
wants to exit without saving.
*/
    inquire_forms form (anychange = change);
    if anychange = 1 then
        answer = prompt 'Changes are not saved.  Do you want to
                         exit?'
            with style = menuline;
        if lowercase (left(answer, 1)) = 'y' then
            return;

        else

            resume;
        endif;
    endif;
    return;
end
```

FIGURE 10.20   *(Continued)*

If you have followed through this chapter you will have completed these frames:

topframe   Main menu for the application.

customer   Maintain customer information.

popcusname   Popup help for customer information.

inventory   Maintain inventory information.

Two more programs complete this sample application: the frame ''salespeople'' used to maintain information on the sales staff, and the frame ''orderentry'' to enter customer orders. The forms and source code for these programs can be found in Appendix C and Appendix D. Create these frames, forms, and source code if you would like to complete the entire sample application.

To create an executable of our application, select **Image** from the Utility menu option on the ABF - Edit an Application screen. To run your completed application from the operating system, use the following command:

imagename [-ddatabase] [framename]

Appendix A

SQL SUMMARY OF COMMANDS, DATA TYPES, AND FUNCTIONS

COMMIT	**DROP**	**MODIFY**
COPY	**DROP INTEGRITY**	**ROLLBACK**
CREATE INDEX	**DROP PERMIT**	**SAVE**
CREATE INTEGRITY	**DROP PROCEDURE**	**SAVEPOINT**
CREATE PROCEDURE	**GRANT**	**SELECT**
CREATE TABLE	**HELP**	**SET**
CREATE VIEW	**INSERT**	**UPDATE**
DELETE		

data types	**set_functions**	**type_functions**
numeric_functions	**string_functions**	

COMMIT. Commit the current transaction.
The syntax of the COMMIT statement is:

COMMIT [WORK]

The optional word WORK has no effect. It is included for compatibility with other versions of SQL.

Examples:

insert into salespeople (lname, partno, salesno)
values (''Williams'', 8111, 4002);
commit;

COPY. Copy data from/into a table from/into a file.
The syntax of the COPY statement is:

COPY TABLE table-name
(column-name = format [WITH NULL (value)]
{, column-name = format [WITH NULL (value)]})
INTO | FROM 'file_specification'
[WITH with_clause]

Examples:

copy table salespeople (lname = vchar(10), fname = vchar(10))
from 'myfile.in';

copy table employee (lname = vchar(10), fname = vchar(10))
into 'myfile.out,text';

CREATE INDEX. Create an index on an existing base table.
The syntax of a CREATE INDEX statement is:

CREATE [UNIQUE] INDEX indexname ON tablename
(columnname [ASC | DESC] {, columnname [ASC | DESC]})
[WITH with_clause]

Examples:

create index invidx on inventory (partno);
create index salesidx on salespeople (salesno, partno);

CREATE INTEGRITY. Define integrity constraints on a base table. Supported when INGRES is used over a network, rather than PC based.
The syntax of a CREATE INTEGRITY statement is:

CREATE INTEGRITY ON tablename IS qualification ;

Examples:

create integrity on inventory is partno in (9111, 9112, 9113, 9114, 9115);

create integrity on inventory is qty > 0 and qty < 10000;

CREATE PROCEDURE. Create a named database procedure definition. Supported when INGRES is used over a network, rather than PC based.
The syntax of a CREATE PROCEDURE statement is:

[CREATE] PROCEDURE proc_name
[(param_name [=] param_type {,param_name[=] param_type})]
= | AS
[declare_section]
BEGIN
statement {;statement} [;]
END;

Examples:

```
create procedure mark_emp
(id INTEGER NOT NULL, label VARCHAR(100)) AS
  BEGIN
    update salespeople
    set comment = :label
    where id = :id;
    if iirowcount = 1 then
      message 'Salespeople was marked'
      commit;
      return 1;
    else
      message 'Salespeople was not marked - record error'
      rollback;
      return 0;
      endif;
  end;
```

CREATE TABLE. Create a new base table.
The syntax of a CREATE TABLE statement is:

```
CREATE TABLE tablename
[(columnname [format] {,columnname [format]})]
[AS sub-select]
[WITH with_clause]
```

When running under INGRES/STAR, the following additional syntax applies:

```
CREATE TABLE linkname
[(columnname [format] {,columnname [format]})]
[AS sub-select]
  [
      WITH
      [NODE = nodename, DATABASE = databasename,]
      [LOCATION    =          location,]
      [TABLE       =          tablename,]
      [JOURNALING | NOJOURNALING]
  ]
```

Examples:

```
create table sample1 (col1 integer4, col2 vchar(6), col3 float8);

create table sample1 as
select partno, qty, cost
from inventory
where cost > avg(cost);
```

CREATE VIEW. Define a virtual table.
The syntax of a CREATE VIEW statement is:

CREATE VIEW viewname
[(columnname {, columnname})]
AS sub-select
[**WITH CHECK OPTION**]

Examples:

create view pcolors (partno, description)
as select partno, description
from inventory;
create view notparis
as select *
from salespeople
where salesno not in
(select salesno from salespeople where salesofc = ''Phoenix'');

DELETE. Delete rows from a table.
The syntax of a DELETE statement is:

DELETE FROM tablename [corr_name]
[**WHERE search_condition**]

Examples:

delete from inventory where inventory.partno = 9111;

delete from inventory; (deletes all rows from p)

delete from salespeople where salesno in
(select salesno from salespeople where salesofc = ''Phoenix'');

delete from inventory where cost between 1 and 13;

DROP. Destroy one or more tables, indexes, or views.
The syntax of a DROP statement is:

DROP tablename|indexname|viewname
    {, **tablename|indexname|viewname**}

Alternate forms:

DROP INDEX indexname {, indexname}
DROP TABLE tablename {, tablename}
DROP VIEW viewname {, viewname}

Examples:

drop inventory, salespeople;

DROP INTEGRITY. Destroy one or more integrity constraints. Supported when INGRES is used over a network, rather than PC based.
The syntax of a DROP INTEGRITY statement is:

DROP INTEGRITY ON tablename integer {, integer} | ALL

---

where the integer arguments are those displayed by a "HELP INTEGRITY tablename" statement.

Example:

drop integrity on salespeople 0, 4, 5;

DROP PERMIT. Destroy one or more permissions. Supported when INGRES is used over a network, rather than PC based.
The syntax of a DROP PERMIT statement for tables and views is:

DROP PERMIT ON tablename
integer {, integer} | ALL

For procedures:

DROP PERMIT ON PROCEDURE proc_name
integer | ALL

where the integer arguments are those displayed by a "HELP PERMIT tablename" statement.

Examples:

drop permit on salespeople all;

drop permit on procedure my_procedure 2;

DROP PROCEDURE. Remove a procedure definition from the database. Supported when INGRES is used over a network, rather than PC based.
The syntax of a DROP PROCEDURE statement is:

DROP PROCEDURE proc_name

Example:

drop procedure my_procedure;

GRANT. Grant privileges on a table, view, or procedure. Supported when INGRES is used over a network, rather than PC based.
The syntax of the GRANT statement is:

GRANT {priv{,priv} | ALL [PRIVILEGES]}
ON [TABLE] tablename {,tablename}
TO username{,username} | PUBLIC

GRANT EXECUTE ON PROCEDURE proc_name
TO username{, username} | PUBLIC

where "priv" represents one of the following privileges:
select
insert
delete
update (columnname{,columnname})

Examples:

> **grant all on mytable to public;**
> **grant update (col1) on mytable to yourname;**

HELP. Get information about tables, views, permits, or integrities.
The syntax of the help command is:

> **HELP [ALL | tablename {, tablename}]**
> **HELP VIEW viewname {, viewname}**
> **HELP PERMIT tablename {, tablename}**
> **HELP INTEGRITY tablename {, tablename}**

The following additional options are available only when running under INGRES/ STAR:

> **HELP LINK [ALL | linkname {, linkname}]**
> **HELP NODE [ALL | nodename {, nodename}]**
> **HELP VIEW [ALL | viewname {, viewname}]**

Examples:

> **help all;**
> **help view salespeople, lname;**
> **help integrity salespeople;**
> **help permit inventory, cost;**

INSERT. Insert rows into a table.
The syntax of an INSERT statement is:

> **INSERT INTO tablename [(column {, column})]**
> **[VALUES (expression {, expression}) | subquery]**

Examples:

> **insert into salespeople (salesno, partno, salesofc)**
> **values (4002,8111,"Phoenix");**
>
> **insert into sample (salesno)**
> **select salesno from salespeople where salesofc = "Phoenix" or salesno > 3000;**

MODIFY. Convert the storage structure of a table or index.
The syntax of a MODIFY statement is:

> **MODIFY tablename|indexname TO**
> **storage_structure | MERGE | RELOCATE | REORGANIZE |**
> **TRUNCATED**
> **[UNIQUE]**
> **[ON column [ASC|DESC] {, column [ASC|DESC]}]**
> **[WITH with_clause]**

Examples:

> **modify inventory to isam on partno;**
>
> **modify sample to chash on salesno, partno with salesofc = "Phoenix";**

ROLLBACK. Roll back the current transaction.
The syntax of the ROLLBACK statement is:

ROLLBACK [WORK] [TO savepoint]

The optional word WORK has no effect. It is included for compatibility with other versions of SQL.

Examples:

> **insert into salespeople (lname, fname, salesno)**
> **values ("Jones", "Juan", 1009);**
> **savepoint lastsave;**
> **insert into salespeople (lname, fname, salesno)**
> **values ("Jones", "John", 1009);**
> **rollback to lastsave;**

SAVE. Save a base table until a specified date.
The syntax of the SAVE statement is:

SAVE tablename UNTIL month day year;

Examples:

> **save mytable until 12 27 1982;**

> **save yourtable until JAN 1 1985;**

SAVEPOINT. Declare a savepoint marker within a transaction. Supported when INGRES is used over a network, rather than PC based.
The syntax of the SAVEPOINT statement is:

SAVEPOINT savepoint_name ;

Example:

> **insert into salespeople (lname, fname, salesno)**
> **values ("Jones", "Juan", 1009);**
> **savepoint lastsave;**
> **insert into salespeople (lname, fname, salesno)**
> **values ("Jones", "Juan", 1009);**
> **rollback to lastsave;**

SELECT. Select data from the database for display onscreen.
The syntax of a SELECT statement is:

> **sub-select {UNION sub-select}**
> **[ORDER BY column [ASC|DESC]**
> **{,column [ASC|DESC]}];**

where a sub-select has the syntax:

> **SELECT . . .**
> **FROM . . .**
> **[WHERE search_condition]**

[GROUP BY . . .]
[HAVING search_condition]

Examples:

    select partno, salesno from sample;

    select x.partno, y.salesno from inventory x, salespeople y
    where x.description = 'wrench';

    select sum(qty), partno
    from sample
    where salesno ! = 2001
    group by partno;

SET. Set INGRES session option.
The syntax of a SET statement is:

    SET AUTOCOMMIT ON | OFF
    SET JOURNALING | NOJOURNALING [ON tablename]
    SET RESULT_STRUCTURE "HEAP | CHEAP | HEAPSORT |
        CHEAPSORT | HASH | CHASH | ISAM | CISAM | BTREE | CBTREE"

    SET LOCKMODE SESSION | ON tablename
        WHERE [LEVEL = PAGE | TABLE | SESSION | SYSTEM]
        [, READLOCK = NOLOCK | SHARED | EXCLUSIVE | SESSION |
        SYSTEM]
        [, MAXLOCKS = n | SESSION | SYSTEM]
        [, TIMEOUT = n | SESSION | SYSTEM]

UPDATE. Update values of columns in a table.
The syntax of an UPDATE statement is:

    UPDATE tablename [corr_name]
    SET column = expression {, column = expression}
    [WHERE search_condition];

Examples:

    update inventory set qty = qty/2 where partno = 9111;

    update inventory set qty = sqrt(qty) where salesno in
    (select salesno from salespeople where salesofc = "Phoenix");

Data types. SQL valid data types.

SQL data types include:

    Abstract: **date**

                   money

    Character: **char**

                   c

	varchar	
	vchar	
Numeric:	**float**	(same as float8)
	float4	
	float8	
	integer	
	integer1	
	integer2	(same as smallint)
	integer4	(same as integer)
	smallint	

Numeric_functions. Functions on numeric values include:

abs(n)

atan(n)

cos(n)

exp(n)

log(n)

mod(n, b)

sin(n)

sqrt(n)

Set_functions. Functions on sets of values include:

COUNT({[DISTINCT | ALL] column_name} | *)

SUM([DISTINCT | ALL]column_name)

AVG([DISTINCT | ALL]column_name)

MIN(column_name)

MAX(column_name)

String_functions. Functions on string variables include:

concat(string1, string2)

left(string1, length)

length(string)

locate(string1, string2)

lowercase(string)

pad(string)

right(string, length)

shift(string, n_places)

size(string)

squeeze(string)

trim(string)

uppercase (string)

Type_functions. Functions to convert between data types include:

ascii(expr)

c(expr)

char(expr)

date(expr)

dow(expr)   convert absolute day to day of week

float4(expr)

float8(expr)

hex(expr)

int1(expr)

int2(expr)

int4(expr)

interval(x, y)

money(expr)

varchar(expr)

vchar(expr)

Appendix B

QUEL SUMMARY OF COMMANDS, DATA TYPES, AND FUNCTIONS

ABORT	DELETE	PRINT
APPEND	DESTROY	RANGE
BEGIN TRANSACTION	DESTROY INTEGRITY	REPLACE
COPY	DESTROY PERMIT	RETRIEVE
CREATE	END TRANSACTION	SAVE
DEFINE INTEGRITY	HELP	SAVEPOINT
DEFINE PERMIT	INDEX	SET
DEFINE VIEW	MODIFY	

data types	set_functions
type_functions	
numeric_functions	string_functions

ABORT. Undo some or all of a multistatement transaction. Supported when INGRES is used over a network, rather than PC based.
The syntax of the ABORT statement is:

    ABORT [TO savepoint_name]

Examples:

> **begin transaction**
> **append to salespeople (lname = "Williams", salesno = 10004, partno = 1119)**
> **abort**

> **begin transaction**
> **append to salespeople (lname = "Williams", salesno = 1004, partno = 9111)**
> **savepoint lastsave**
> **append to salespeople (lname = "Shahmohamadi", salesno = 1006, partno = 9112)**
> **abort to lastsave**

APPEND. Insert rows into a table.
The syntax of an APPEND statement is:

> **APPEND TO tablelname**
> **([column =] expression {, [column =] expression})**

> **[WHERE qualification]**

Examples:

> **append to salespeople (lname = "Williams", fname = "Chauncey",**
> **salesno = 1004**
> **partno = "5115", salesofc = "Phoenix")**

> **append to sample (salespeople.all)**
> **where salespeople.salesofc = "Las Vegas" or salespeople.salesofc = "San Diego"**

BEGIN TRANSACTION. Declare start of multistatement transaction. Supported when INGRES is used over a network, rather than PC based.
The syntax of the BEGIN TRANSACTION statement is:

> **BEGIN TRANSACTION**

Example:

> **begin transaction**
> **append to salespeople (lname = "Jones", salesno = 1007, partno = 8119)**
> **append to salespeople (lname = "Smith", salesno = 3002, partno = 8111)**
> **end transaction**

COPY. Copy date from/into a table from/into a file.
The syntax of the COPY statement is:

> **COPY tablename**
> **(columnname = format [WITH NULL (value)]**
> **{, columnname = format [WITH NULL (value)]})**
> **INTO | FROM "file_specification"**
> **[WITH with_clause]**

Examples:

    **copy salespeople (lname = text(10), fname = text(10), partno = i2)
from "myfile.in";**

    copy salespeople (lname = text(10), partno = i2) into "myfile.out";

CREATE. Create a new base table.
The syntax of a CREATE statement is:

    **CREATE tablename
[(column = format {, column = format})]**

    [WITH with_clause]

Example:

    **create sample (salesno = i2, partno = i2, cusno = i2, salesofc = c12, lname =
"Williams")**

DEFINE INTEGRITY. Define integrity constraints on a base table. Supported when
INGRES is used over a network, rather than PC based.
The syntax of a DEFINE INTEGRITY statement is:

    DEFINE INTEGRITY ON rangevar IS qualification

Examples:

    **define integrity on inventory is inventory.partno = 9111 or
inventory.partno = 9112 or inventory.partno = 9113 or
inventory.partno = 9114 or inventory.partno = 9115**

    **define integrity on inventory is inventory.qty > 0 and
inventory.qty < 10000**

DEFINE PERMIT. Define permissions for a base table. Supported when INGRES is
used over a network, rather than PC based.
The syntax of a DEFINE PERMIT statement is:

    **DEFINE PERMIT oplist {ON | OF | TO} rangevar
[(columnlname {, columnlname})]
TO user_lname
[AT terminal]
[FROM time TO time]
[ON day TO day]
[WHERE search_condition]**

Example:

    define permit retrieve, replace, append on test to johndoe

DEFINE VIEW. Define a virtual table.
The syntax of a DEFINE VIEW statement is:

DEFINE VIEW viewlname
([column =] expression {, [column =] expression})

[WHERE qualification]

Examples:

define view icolors (inventory.partno, inventory.description)

define view notphoenix (salespeople.all)
where any (salespeople.salesofc by sample.salesofc
where salespeople.salesofc = sample.salesofc and sample.salesofc
= ''Phoenix'') = 0

DELETE. Delete rows from a table.
The syntax of a DELETE statement is:

DELETE rangevar
[WHERE search _ condition]

Examples:

delete inventory where inventory.partno = ''9111''

delete salespeople

(deletes all rows from salespeople)

delete inventory where inventory.salesno = salespeople.salesno and
salespeople.salesofc = ''Phoenix''

delete salespeople where 1000 < = salespeople.salesno and salespeople.salesno
< = 3001

DESTROY. Destroy one or more tables, indexes, or views.
The syntax of a DESTROY statement is:

DESTROY tablelname|indexlname|viewlname
{, tablelname|indexlname|viewlname }

Example:

destroy salespeople, inventory

DESTROY INTEGRITY. Destroy one or more integrity constraints. Supported when INGRES is used over a network, rather than PC based.
The syntax of a DESTROY INTEGRITY statement is:

DESTROY INTEGRITY tablename integer {, integer } | ALL

where the integer arguments are those displayed by a ''HELP INTEGRITY tablename'' statement.

Example:

destroy integrity job 0, 4, 5

DESTROY PERMIT. Destroy one or more permissions. Supported when INGRES is used over a network, rather than PC based.

The syntax of a DESTROY PERMIT statement is:

DESTROY PERMIT tablelname
integer {, integer} | ALL

where the integer arguments are those displayed by a "HELP PERMIT tablelname" statement.

Example:

destroy permit job all

END TRANSACTION. Stop in-progress transaction, and commit its replaces to the database. Supported when INGRES is used over a network, rather than PC based.

The syntax of the END TRANSACTION statement is:

END TRANSACTION

Example:

begin transaction
append to salespeople (lname = "Jones", salesno = 10000, partno = 1923)
append to salespeople (lname = "Smith", salesno = 23000, partno = 1943)
end transaction

HELP. Get information about tables, views, permits, or integrities.

The syntax of the HELP command is:

HELP [ALL | tablelname {, tablelname}]
HELP VIEW viewlname {, viewlname}
HELP PERMIT tablelname {, tablelname}
HELP INTEGRITY tablelname {, tablelname}

Examples:

help all
help view job, salespeople
help integrity job
help permit salespeople, dept

INDEX. Create an index on an existing base table.

The syntax of an INDEX statement is:

INDEX [UNIQUE] ON tablelname IS
[locationlname:]indexlname
(columnlname {, columnlname})

Examples:

index on salespeople is slsx (partno)

index on inventory is invx (salesno, partno)

MODIFY. Convert the storage structure of a table or index.
The syntax of a MODIFY statement is:

MODIFY tablename|indexlname TO
storage_structure | MERGE | RELOCATE | REORGANIZE |
TRUNCATED
[UNIQUE]
　　[ON COLUMN [:ASCENDING|DESCENDING]
　　{, column [:ASCENDING|DESCENDING]}]
　　[WITH with_clause]

Examples:

modify salespeople to isam on partno;
modify salespeople to chash on salesno, partno with minpages = 16;

PRINT. Print table(s).
The syntax of a PRINT statement is:

PRINT tablelname {,tablelname}

Examples:

print my_tablelname
print my_tablelname, your_tablelname

RANGE. Declare a range variable.
The syntax of a RANGE statement is:

RANGE of range_var IS tablename {, range_var IS tablelname}

Example:

range of x is salespeople, y is inventory

A tablename itself is also considered a valid rangevar as if declared by the statement:

range of tablename is tablename

REPLACE. Update values of columns in a table.
The syntax of a REPLACE statement is:

REPLACE rangevar
(column = expression {, column = expression})
[WHERE search_condition]

Examples:

replace inventory (qty = inventory.qty/2) where
inventory.partno = 9111

replace inventory (qty = sqrt(inventory.qty)) where
inventory.partno =
salespeople.partno and salespeople.salesofc = ''Phoenix''

RETRIEVE. Select data from the database for display onscreen.
The syntax of a RETRIEVE statement is:

RETRIEVE [INTO tablename|UNIQUE]
([column =] expression {, [column =] expression})
[WHERE search_condition]
[SORT [BY] column[:ASCENDING|DESCENDING]
{, column[:ASCENDING|DESCENDING]}]
[ORDER [BY] column[:ASCENDING|DESCENDING]
{, column[:ASCENDING|DESCENDING]}]
[WITH with_clause]

Examples:

retrieve (inventory.partno, salespeople.salesno)

range of x is inventory, y is salespeople
retrieve (x.partno, y.salesno)
where x.cost < 12

retrieve (inventory.partno, salespeople = sum(inventory.qty by
inventory. partno where inventory.price > 5.50))
where inventory.price > 5.50

SAVE. Save a base table until a specified date.
The syntax of the SAVE statement is:

SAVE tablename UNTIL month day year

Examples:

save mytable until 12 27 1982
save yourtable until JAN 1 1985

SAVEPOINT. Declare a savepoint marker within a transaction. Supported when INGRES is used over a network, rather than PC based.
The syntax of the SAVEPOINT statement is:

SAVEPOINT savepoint_lname

Example:

begin transaction
append to salespeople (lname = "Williams", salesno = 1004, partno = 9111)
savepoint lastsave
append to salespeople (lname = "Shahmohamadi", salesno = 1006, partno =
9112)
abort to lastsave

SET. Set INGRES session option.
The syntax of a SET statement is:

SET JOURNALING | NOJOURNALING [ON tablename]

SET JOINOP | NOJOINOP
SET RET_INTO "HEAP | CHEAP | HEAPSORT | CHEAPSORT |
          HASH | CHASH | ISAM | CISAM | BTREE |
          CBTREE"
  SET LOCKMODE SESSION | ON tablename
    WHERE [LEVEL = PAGE | TABLE | SESSION | SYSTEM]
  [, READLOCK = NOLOCK | SHARED | EXCLUSIVE | SESSION |
  SYSTEM]
  [, MAXLOCKS = n | SESSION | SYSTEM]
  [, TIMEOUT = n | SESSION | SYSTEM]

Data types. QUEL valid data types.

QUEL data types include:

cn   (n is the maximum character length) **text(n)** (n is
                              the maximum text length)

i4

i2

i1

f8

f4

date

money

Set_functions. Functions on sets of values include:

COUNT(column_lname)

COUNTU(column_lname)

SUM(column_lname)

SUMU(column_lname)

AVG(column_lname)

AVGU(column_lname)

MIN(column_lname)

MAX(column_lname)

Numeric_functions. Functions on numeric values include:

abs(n)

atan(n)

cos(n)

exp(n)

log(n)

mod(n, b)

sin(n)

sqrt(n)

Type_functions. Functions to convert between data types include:

ascii(expr)

date(expr)

dow(expr)   convert absolute day to day of week

float4(expr)

float8(expr)

int1(expr)

int2(expr)

int4(expr)

interval(x, y)

money(expr)

text(expr)

String_functions. Functions on string variables include:

concat(string1, string2)

left(string1, length)

length(string)

locate(string1, string2)

lowercase(string)

pad(string)

right(string, length)

shift(string, n_places)

size(string)

squeeze(string)

money(expr)

text(expr)

String_functions. Functions on string variables include:

concat(string1, string2)

left(string1, length)

length(string)

locate(string1, string2)

lowercase(string)

pad(string)

right(string, length)

shift(string, n_places)

size(string)

squeeze(string)

trim(string)

uppercase(string)

Appendix C

ABF FORMS AND ATTRIBUTES FOR THE APPLICATION "SAMPLE"

This appendix contains detailed information about the forms used in the application "Sample." This information was created using the INGRES operating system command Printform. The forms for salespeople and orderentry can be found here. These are the two frames that were not created in Chapter 10. Use the forms description in the appendix along with the code found in Appendix D to create these additional frames.

FIGURE C.1 *Topframe Form*

```
┌──────────────────────────────────────────────────────────────┐
│              ARIZONA WIDGET WHOLESALE SUPPLY COMPANY           │
│                     234 N. CENTRAL AVENUE                      │
│                    PHOENIX, ARIZONA 85001                      │
│                        602-251-6000                           │
│                                                               │
│        ┌───────────────────────────────────────────────┐     │
│        │                                                 │     │
│        │                  Main Menu                      │     │
│        │                                                 │     │
│        │      (1)   Enter customer orders                │     │
│        │      (2)   Maintain customer information         │     │
│        │      (3)   Maintain inventory                    │     │
│        │      (4)   Maintain sales staff information      │     │
│        │                                                 │     │
│        │                                                 │     │
│        └───────────────────────────────────────────────┘     │
│                                                               │
│                                                               │
│                                                               │
│                                                               │
└──────────────────────────────────────────────────────────────┘
```

FIGURE C.2 *Topframe Form Description*

Form name: topframe
Form owner: <Username>
Form Display Style is: FullScreen.
Number of columns on screen: 80
Number of lines on screen: 22
Number of fields: 0
Number of trim strings: 10
Date first created: 1990_01_03 04:06:27 GMT
Date last modified: 1990_02_03 18:03:00 GMT

FIELD DESCRIPTIONS

TRIM DESCRIPTIONS

Box trim at row '7' and column '12' is '11' rows high and '55' columns wide.
Foreground display color number is: '0'
Special display attributes: Reverse video

Text trim at row '2' and column '21' is:
    'ARIZONA WIDGET WHOLESALE SUPPLY COMPANY'.
Foreground display color number is: '0'
Special display attributes: None

Text trim at row '9' and column '34' is:
    'Main Menu'.
Foreground display color number is: '0'
Special display attributes: None

FIGURE C.2 *continued*

Text trim at row '11' and column '22' is:
    '(1)   Enter customer orders'.
Foreground display color number is: '0'
Special display attributes: None

Text trim at row '12' and column '22' is:
    '(2)   Maintain customer information'.
Foreground display color number is: '0'
Special display attributes: None

Text trim at row '13' and column '22' is:
    '(3)   Maintain inventory'.
Foreground display color number is: '0'
Special display attributes: None

Text trim at row '14' and column '22' is:
    '(4)   Maintain sales staff information'.
Foreground display color number is: '0'
Special display attributes: None

Text trim at row '4' and column '29' is:
    'PHOENIX, ARIZONA 85001'.
Foreground display color number is: '0'
Special display attributes: None

Text trim at row '3' and column '30' is:
    '234 N. CENTRAL AVENUE'.
Foreground display color number is: '0'
Special display attributes: None

Text trim at row '5' and column '34' is:
    '602-251-6000'.
Foreground display color number is: '0'
Special display attributes: None

FIGURE C.3 *Popcusname Form*

Number	Customer Name	Address	Phone

FIGURE C.4 *Popcusname Form Description*

```
Form name: popcusname
Form owner: <Username>
Form Display style is: Floating popup.
Form has borders disabled.
Number of columns on screen: 73
Number of lines on screen: 12
Number of fields: 1
Number of trim strings: 0
Date first created: 1990_02_03 17:31:11 GMT
Date last modified: 1990_02_03 19:31:29 GMT


FIELD DESCRIPTIONS


Table field name: customer
Number of rows in table field: 8
Special table field attributes: No row separators, Highlighting current row enabl


Column name: cusno
Column title: Number
Data type: Non-nullable  i2
Display format: -i4
Foreground display color number is: '0'
Special display attributes: None
Type of field: column in table field
Default value:
Validation check:
Validation error message:

Column name: cusname
Column title:       Customer Name
Data type: Non-nullable  char(25)
Display format: c25
Foreground display color number is: '0'
Special display attributes: None
Type of field: column in table field
Default value:
Validation check:
Validation error message:


Column name: cusaddress
Column title:        Address
Data type: Non-nullable  char(25)
Display format: c25
Foreground display color number is: '0'
Special display attributes: None
Type of field: column in table field
Default value:
Validation check:
Validation error message:
```

FIGURE C.4 *continued*

```
Column name: cusphone
Column title:     Phone
Data type: Non-nullable  char(12)
Display format: c12
Foreground display color number is: '0'
Special display attributes: None
Type of field: column in table field
Default value:
Validation check:
Validation error message:
```

TRIM DESCRIPTIONS

FIGURE C.5 *Orderentry Form*

```
                    MAINTAIN CUSTOMER ORDERS
                Arizona Widget Wholesale Supply Company


     Customer Number:          Customer Name:
              Address:
                 City:
                State:              Zip:
                Phone:

        ┌───────────┬─────┬──────────┬─────────────┬────┬────────┐
        │Salespeople│Part │Order Date│Delivery Date│Qty │ Price  │
        ├───────────┼─────┼──────────┼─────────────┼────┼────────┤
        │           │     │          │             │    │        │
        │           │     │          │             │    │        │
        │           │     │          │             │    │        │
        │           │     │          │             │    │        │
        │           │     │          │             │    │        │
        └───────────┴─────┴──────────┴─────────────┴────┴────────┘
```

FIGURE C.6 *Orderentry Form Description*

```
Form name: orderentry
Form owner: <Username>
Form Display Style is: FullScreen.
Number of columns on screen: 80
Number of lines on screen: 22
Number of fields: 8
Number of trim strings: 2
Date first created: 1990_02_03 21:37:55 GMT
Date last modified: 1990_02_10 16:50:01 GMT
```

FIGURE C.6 *continued*

FIELD DESCRIPTIONS

Field name: cusno
Field title: Customer Number:
Data type: Non-nullable i2
Display format: -i4
Foreground display color number is: '0'
Special display attributes: Underline
Type of field: regular
Default value:
Validation check:
Validation error message:

Field name: cusname
Field title: Customer Name:
Data type: Non-nullable char(25)
Display format: c25
Foreground display color number is: '0'
Special display attributes: Display only
Type of field: regular
Default value:
Validation check:
Validation error message:

Field name: cusaddress
Field title: Address:
Data type: Non-nullable char(25)
Display format: c25
Foreground display color number is: '0'
Special display attributes: Display only
Type of field: regular
Default value:
Validation check:
Validation error message:

Field name: cuscity
Field title: City:
Data type: Non-nullable char(25)
Display format: c25
Foreground display color number is: '0'
Special display attributes: Display only
Type of field: regular
Default value:
Validation check:
Validation error message:

Field name: cusstate
Field title: State:
Data type: Non-nullable char(2)
Display format: c2
Foreground display color number is: '0'
Special display attributes: Display only
Type of field: regular
Default value:
Validation check:
Validation error message:

FIGURE C.6 *continued*

Field name: cuszip
Field title: Zip:
Data type: Non-nullable char(5)
Display format: c5
Foreground display color number is: '0'
Special display attributes: Display only
Type of field: regular
Default value:
Validation check:
Validation error message:

Field name: cusphone
Field title: Phone:
Data type: Non-nullable char(12)
Display format: c12
Foreground display color number is: '0'
Special display attributes: Display only
Type of field: regular
Default value:
Validation check:
Validation error message:

Table field name: transtbl
Number of rows in table field: 8
Special table field attributes: No row separators

Column name: salesno
Column title: Salespeople
Data type: Non-nullable i2
Display format: +i4
Foreground display color number is: '0'
Special display attributes: None
Type of field: column in table field
Default value:
Validation check:
Validation error message:

Column name: partno
Column title: Part
Data type: Non-nullable i2
Display format: +i4
Foreground display color number is: '0'
Special display attributes: None
Type of field: column in table field
Default value:
Validation check:
Validation error message:

Column name: date
Column title: Order Date
Data type: Non-nullable date
Display format: d"2/3/1"
Foreground display color number is: '0'
Special display attributes: None

FIGURE C.6 *continued*

```
Type of field: column in table field
Default value:
Validation check:
Validation error message:


Column name: deldate
Column title: Delivery Date
Data type: Non-nullable  date
Display format: d"2/3/1"
Foreground display color number is: '0'
Special display attributes: None
Type of field: column in table field
Default value:
Validation check:
Validation error message:


Column name: qty
Column title: Qty
Data type: Non-nullable  i2
Display format: +i4
Foreground display color number is: '0'
Special display attributes: None
Type of field: column in table field
Default value:
Validation check:
Validation error message:


Column name: ordrprice
Column title:  Price
Data type: Non-nullable  money
Display format: +"$-----.nn"
Foreground display color number is: '0'
Special display attributes: Display only
Type of field: column in table field
Default value:
Validation check:
Validation error message:




TRIM DESCRIPTIONS


Text trim at row '1' and column '21' is:
     'Arizona Widget Wholesale Supply Company'.
Foreground display color number is: '0'
Special display attributes: None


Text trim at row '0' and column '26' is:
     'MAINTAIN CUSTOMER ORDERS'.
Foreground display color number is: '0'
Special display attributes: None
```

FIGURE C.7 *Customer Form*

```
                    MAINTAIN CUSTOMER INFORMATION
                  Arizona Widget Wholesale Supply Company


       Customer Number:

         Customer Name:

               Address:

                  City:

                 State:                    Zip:

                 Phone:




```

FIGURE C.8 *Customer Form Description*

Form name: customer
Form owner: <Username>
Form Display Style is: FullScreen.
Number of columns on screen: 80
Number of lines on screen: 22
Number of fields: 7
Number of trim strings: 2
Date first created: 1990_01_03 04:34:02 GMT
Date last modified: 1990_02_03 19:30:37 GMT

FIELD DESCRIPTIONS

Field name: cusno
Field title: Customer Number:
Data type: Non-nullable   i2
Display format: -i4
Foreground display color number is: '0'
Special display attributes: Reverse video
Type of field: regular
Default value:
Validation check:
Validation error message:

Field name: cusname
Field title: Customer Name:
Data type: Non-nullable   char(25)
Display format: c25
Foreground display color number is: '0'
Special display attributes: Mandatory field, Reverse video
Type of field: regular
Default value:

FIGURE C.8 *continued*

```
Validation check:
Validation error message:


Field name: cusaddress
Field title: Address:
Data type: Non-nullable  char(25)
Display format: c25
Foreground display color number is: '0'
Special display attributes: Reverse video
Type of field: regular
Default value:
Validation check:
Validation error message:

Field name: cuscity
Field title: City:
Data type: Non-nullable  char(25)
Display format: c25
Foreground display color number is: '0'
Special display attributes: Reverse video
Type of field: regular
Default value:
Validation check:
Validation error message:


Field name: cusstate
Field title: State:
Data type: Non-nullable  char(2)
Display format: c2
Foreground display color number is: '0'
Special display attributes: Reverse video, Force upper case
Type of field: regular
Default value:
Validation check:
Validation error message:


Field name: cuszip
Field title: Zip:
Data type: Non-nullable  char(5)
Display format: c5
Foreground display color number is: '0'
Special display attributes: Reverse video
Type of field: regular
Default value:
Validation check:
Validation error message:


Field name: cusphone
Field title: Phone:
Data type: Non-nullable  char(12)
Display format: c12
Foreground display color number is: '0'
Special display attributes: Reverse video
Type of field: regular
Default value:
```

FIGURE C.8 *continued*

Validation check:
Validation error message:

TRIM DESCRIPTIONS

Text trim at row '1' and column '21' is:
     'Arizona Widget Wholesale Supply Company'.
Foreground display color number is: '0'
Special display attributes: None

Text trim at row '0' and column '26' is:
     'MAINTAIN CUSTOMER INFORMATION'.
Foreground display color number is: '0'
Special display attributes: None

FIGURE C.9 *Inventory Form*

```
+--------------------------------------------------------------------------+
|                    MAINTAIN INVENTORY INFORMATION                        |
|                 Arizona Widget Wholesale Supply Company                  |
|                                                                          |
|   +--------+----+----------------------------+--------+------+-------+    |
|   | Number |Qty |        Description          | Reorder| Cost | Price |   |
|   +--------+----+----------------------------+--------+------+-------+   |
|   |        |    |                            |        |      |       |   |
|   |        |    |                            |        |      |       |   |
|   |        |    |                            |        |      |       |   |
|   |        |    |                            |        |      |       |   |
|   |        |    |                            |        |      |       |   |
|   |        |    |                            |        |      |       |   |
|   |        |    |                            |        |      |       |   |
|   +--------+----+----------------------------+--------+------+-------+   |
|                                                                          |
+--------------------------------------------------------------------------+
```

FIGURE C.10 *Inventory Form Description*

Form name: inventory
Form owner: <Username>
Form Display Style is: FullScreen.
Number of columns on screen: 82
Number of lines on screen: 21
Number of fields: 1
Number of trim strings: 2
Date first created: 1990_02_03 19:50:59 GMT
Date last modified: 1990_02_03 21:01:55 GMT

FIGURE C.10 *continued*

FIELD DESCRIPTIONS

```
Table field name: inventorytbl
Number of rows in table field: 12
Special table field attributes: No row separators


Column name: partno
Column title: Number
Data type: Non-nullable  i2
Display format: +i4
Foreground display color number is: '0'
Special display attributes: None
Type of field: column in table field
Default value:
Validation check:
Validation error message:


Column name: qty
Column title: Qty
Data type: Non-nullable  i2
Display format: +"zzzz"
Foreground display color number is: '0'
Special display attributes: None
Type of field: column in table field
Default value:
Validation check:
Validation error message:


Column name: itemname
Column title:          Description
Data type: Non-nullable  char(30)
Display format: c30
Foreground display color number is: '0'
Special display attributes: None
Type of field: column in table field
Default value:
Validation check:
Validation error message:


Column name: reorder
Column title: Reorder
Data type: Non-nullable  i2
Display format: +"zzz"
Foreground display color number is: '0'
Special display attributes: None
Type of field: column in table field
Default value:
Validation check:
Validation error message:


Column name: cost
Column title:  Cost
Data type: Non-nullable  money
```

FIGURE C.10 *continued*

```
Display format: +"$--.nn"
Foreground display color number is: `0'
Special display attributes: None
Type of field: column in table field
Default value:
Validation check:
Validation error message:


Column name: price
Column title: Price
Data type: Non-nullable  money
Display format: +"$--.nn"
Foreground display color number is: `0'
Special display attributes: None
Type of field: column in table field
Default value:
Validation check:
Validation error message:



TRIM DESCRIPTIONS


Text trim at row `2' and column `22' is:
     `Arizona Widget Wholesale Supply Company'.
Foreground display color number is: `0'
Special display attributes: None


Text trim at row `0' and column `26' is:
     `MAINTAIN INVENTORY INFORMATION'.
Foreground display color number is: `0'
Special display attributes: None
```

FIGURE C.11 *Salespeople Form*

```
                    MAINTAIN SALES STAFF INFORMATION
                  Arizona Widget Wholesale Supply Company

   ┌────────┬───────────────┬──────────────────┬──────────────────┐
   │ Number │   Last Name   │    First Name    │     Location     │
   ├────────┼───────────────┼──────────────────┼──────────────────┤
   │        │               │                  │                  │
   │        │               │                  │                  │
   │        │               │                  │                  │
   │        │               │                  │                  │
   │        │               │                  │                  │
   │        │               │                  │                  │
   │        │               │                  │                  │
   │        │               │                  │                  │
   └────────┴───────────────┴──────────────────┴──────────────────┘
```

FIGURE C.12 *Salespeople Form Description*

```
Form name: salespeople
Form owner: <Username>
Form Display Style is: FullScreen.
Number of columns on screen: 79
Number of lines on screen: 22
Number of fields: 1
Number of trim strings: 2
Date first created: 1990_01_03 04:48:58 GMT
Date last modified: 1990_02_03 21:21:22 GMT


FIELD DESCRIPTIONS


Table field name: salesmentbl
Number of rows in table field: 12
Special table field attributes: No row separators


Column name: salesno
Column title: Number
Data type: Non-nullable  i2
Display format: +i4
Foreground display color number is: '0'
Special display attributes: None
Type of field: column in table field
Default value:
Validation check:
Validation error message:


Column name: lname
Column title:      Last Name
```

FIGURE C.12 *continued*

```
Data type: Non-nullable  char(25)
Display format: c20
Foreground display color number is: '0'
Special display attributes: scrollable
Type of field: column in table field
Default value:
Validation check:
Validation error message:


Column name: fname
Column title:      First Name
Data type: Non-nullable  char(25)
Display format: c20
Foreground display color number is: '0'
Special display attributes: scrollable
Type of field: column in table field
Default value:
Validation check:
Validation error message:


Column name: salesofc
Column title:      Location
Data type: Non-nullable  char(25)
Display format: c15
Foreground display color number is: '0'
Special display attributes: scrollable
Type of field: column in table field
Default value:
Validation check:
Validation error message:
```

Appendix D

SOURCE CODE FOR THE APPLICATION "SAMPLE"

FIGURE D.1   *Topframe.OSQ*

```
/*
     Frame: Main Menu for application Sample (topframe.osq)
     Author:
     Purpose:  To allow the user to select the desired option from the
               main menu.
*/

initialize () =
begin

/*
    Set autocommit on, assign keyboard map file.
*/

    commit;
    set autocommit on;

/*
    Set field activation to occur whenever the user moves backward
    out of a field or selects a menu key.  The default is already
    set for field activation to occur whenever the user moves
    forward out of a field.
*/

    set_forms frs (activate (previousfield) = 1,
            activate (menu) = 1);

end

'OrderEntry' =
begin

    callframe orderentry();
end
```

FIGURE D.1 *continued*

```
'Customer' =
begin

    callframe customer();
end

'Inventory' =
begin

    callframe inventory();
end

'Salesmen' =
begin

    callframe salesmen();
end

'Exit', key frskey3 =
begin

/*
    Exit the application.
*/

    exit;
end
```

FIGURE D.2 *Orderentry.OSQ*

```
/*
    Frame:   Maintain Customer Transactions (orderentry.osq)
    Purpose: To  add, change, or delete customers orders from the
                 Order database.
*/

initialize (
    answer                  = char(1)    not null with default,
    anychange               = integer2   not null with default,
    error_no                = integer2   not null with default,
    error_text              = varchar(256)   not null with default,
    hold_cusno              = integer2   not null with default,
    ordrprice               = float4     not null with default,
    price                   = float4     not null with default,
    row_count               = integer2   not null with default,
    transtbl.hold_date      = date       not null with default,
    transtbl.hold_deldate   = date       not null with default,
    transtbl.hold_ordrprice = money      not null with default,
    transtbl.hold_partno    = integer2   not null with default,
    transtbl.hold_qty       = integer2   not null with default,
    transtbl.hold_salesno   = integer2   not null with default,
    transtbl.prev_partno    = integer2   not null with default,
    transtbl.status         = integer2   not null with default,
    row_no                  = integer2   not null with default,
    state                   = integer1   not null with default) =

begin
end
```

```
field 'cusno' =
begin

/*
    If customer number has been entered on the screen, get the
    customer information.

*/

    if (cusno = 0) then
     message 'Use ''Find'' to select customer ...';
     sleep 2;
     resume;
    endif;

    if (cusno = hold_cusno) then
     resume field transtbl;
    endif;

    orderentry = select cusname,
                        cusaddress,
                        cuscity,
                        cusstate,
                cuszip,
                        cusphone
            from customer
            where cusno = :cusno;

    inquire_ingres (row_count = rowcount,
            error_no = errorno);

    if (row_count = 0 or error_no != 0) then
     message 'Customer not found ...';
     sleep 2;
     clear field all;
     resume;

    else
     hold_cusno = :cusno;
    endif;

/*
    Initialize tablefield and select into tablefield.  Use the hidden
    column 'status' to determine when a row has been inserted into the
    tablefield.
*/

    inittable transtbl fill;

    transtbl = select salesno,   hold_salesno = salesno,
                     date,       hold_date = date,
                     partno,     hold_partno = partno,
                     deldate,    hold_deldate = deldate,
                     qty,        hold_qty = qty,
                     ordrprice,  hold_ordrprice = ordrprice,
                     prev_partno = partno,
                     status = 2
            from transactions
                where cusno = :cusno;
```

```
    resume field transtbl;
end

field 'transtbl.partno' =
begin

/*
    If the part number has changed, recalculate the order price.  The
    field transtbl.prev_partno will contain the last value of part number
    on the screen. (Note:  transtbl.hold_partno contains the value of
    part number in the database.
*/

    if (transtbl.partno = transtbl.prev_partno) and (transtbl.qty > 0) then
     resume next;
    endif;

    transtbl.prev_partno = :transtbl.partno;

    orderentry = select price
          from inventory
          where partno = :transtbl.partno;

    inquire_ingres (row_count = rowcount,
                   error_no = errorno);

    if (row_count = 0 or error_no != 0) then
     message 'Part number not found in inventory ...';
     sleep 2;
        transtbl.ordrprice = 0;
     resume field transtbl.partno;
    endif;

    transtbl.ordrprice = (:price * :transtbl.qty);
    resume next;
end


field 'transtbl.qty' =
begin

/*
    Get the inventory price for this part, then calculate the order price.
*/

    orderentry = select price
          from inventory
          where partno = :transtbl.partno;

    inquire_ingres (row_count = rowcount,
                   error_no = errorno);

    if (row_count = 0 or error_no != 0) then
     message 'Part number not found in inventory ...';
     sleep 2;
        transtbl.ordrprice = 0;
     resume field transtbl.partno;
    endif;
```

```
    transtbl.ordrprice = (:price * :transtbl.qty);
    resume next;
end

'Save' =
begin

    message 'Saving ...';

/*
    Remove rows marked for delete first.
*/

    unloadtable transtbl (state = _state)
    begin
     if (state = 4) then
         delete from transactions
         where salesno    = :transtbl.salesno
         and   date       = :transtbl.date
         and   cusno      = :cusno
         and   partno     = :transtbl.partno
         and   deldate    = :transtbl.deldate
         and   qty        = :transtbl.qty
         and   ordrprice = :transtbl.ordrprice;

         inquire_ingres (error_no = errorno);
         if (error_no != 0) then
          message 'Problem deleting row ...';
          sleep 2;
          resume;
         endif;
     endif;
    end;


/*
    Do insert and update to rows.
*/

    unloadtable transtbl (state = _state)
    begin
     if (state = 1 or transtbl.status = 5)  and
        (transtbl.salesno != 0 and transtbl.partno != 0) then
         insert into transactions (salesno,
                                    date,
                                    cusno,
                                    partno,
                                    deldate,
                        qty,
                                    ordrprice)
        values (:transtbl.salesno,
                :transtbl.date,
                :cusno,
              :transtbl.partno,
                :transtbl.deldate,
                :transtbl.qty,
              :transtbl.ordrprice);
```

```
elseif (state = 3 and transtbl.status != 5) and
    (transtbl.salesno != 0 and transtbl.partno != 0) then
     update transactions
     set salesno   = :transtbl.salesno,
     date          = :transtbl.date,
     cusno         = :cusno,
     partno        = :transtbl.partno,
     deldate       = :transtbl.deldate,
     qty           = :transtbl.qty,
     ordrprice = :transtbl.ordrprice
     where salesno = :transtbl.hold_salesno
     and    date      = :transtbl.hold_date
     and    cusno     = :cusno
     and    partno    = :transtbl.hold_partno
     and    deldate   = :transtbl.hold_deldate
     and    qty       = :transtbl.hold_qty
     and    ordrprice = :transtbl.hold_ordrprice;
 endif;

 inquire_ingres (error_no = errorno);
 if (error_no != 0) then
     message 'Problem updating row ...';
     sleep 2;
     resume;
 endif;
end;

/*
    Redisplay details.
*/

    inittable transtbl fill;

    transtbl = select salesno,    hold_salesno = salesno,
                       date,       hold_date = date,
                       partno,     hold_partno = partno,
                       deldate,    hold_deldate = deldate,
                       qty,        hold_qty = qty,
                       ordrprice, hold_ordrprice = ordrprice,
                       prev_partno = partno,
                       status = 2
            from transactions
               where cusno = :cusno;

/*
    Set the screen change flag to indicate changes have been saved.
*/

    set_forms form (change = 0);
    resume field transtbl;
end

'Delete' =
begin

/*
    Verify the delete.  If row is to be deleted from the tablefield,
    set the screen change flag.  The row will be deleted from the
    table  during the 'Save' processing.
```

```
*/

    answer = prompt 'Are you sure you want to delete this row? (y/n)'
     with style = menuline;
    if (uppercase(answer) = 'Y') then
     deleterow transtbl;
     set_forms form (change = 1);

    endif;
end

'Insert' =
begin

/*
    Insert row into tablefield.  Set row status to '5' to indicate this
    will be an insert.
*/

    inquire_forms table '' (row_no = rowno);
    row_no = row_no - 1;
    insertrow transtbl[:row_no];
    transtbl.status = 5;
end

'Find' =
begin

/*
    Provide help window.
*/

    callframe popcusname (cusno = byref(:cusno));

    orderentry = select cusname,
                cusaddress,
                cuscity,
                cusstate,
                cuszip,
                cusphone
            from customer
            where cusno = :cusno;

    inquire_ingres (row_count = rowcount,
                    error_no = errorno);

    if (row_count = 0 or error_no != 0) then

     message 'Customer not found ...';
     sleep 2;
     clear field all;
     resume;

    else
     hold_cusno = :cusno;
    endif;
```

FIGURE D.2 *continued*

```
/*
    Initialize tablefield and select into tablefield.  Use the hidden
    column 'status' to determine when a row has been inserted into the
    tablefield.
*/

    inittable transtbl fill;

    transtbl = select salesno,    hold_salesno = salesno,
                       date,       hold_date = date,
                       partno,     hold_partno = partno,
                       deldate,    hold_deldate = deldate,
                       qty,        hold_qty = qty,
                       ordrprice,  hold_ordrprice = ordrprice,
                       prev_partno = partno,
                       status = 2
            from transactions
                where cusno = :cusno;

    resume field transtbl;
end

'Blank' =
begin

/*
    Blank all fields on the screen.
*/

    clear field all;

end

'Exit', key frskey3 =
begin

/*
    Determine if a row(s) have been deleted from table, rows updated, or
    rows added.  If change was found, make sure user wants to exit without
    saving.
*/

    inquire_forms form (anychange = change);
    if anychange = 1 then
     answer = prompt 'Changes are not saved.  Do you want to exit?'
         with style = menuline;
     if lowercase (left(answer, 1)) = 'y' then
         return;

     else
         resume;
     endif;
    endif;
    return;
end
```

FIGURE D.3   *Customer.OSQ*

```
/*
    Frame:    Maintain Customer Information
    Purpose: To   add, change, or delete customers from the
         Order database.
*/

initialize (
    answer      = char(1)      not null with default,
    error_no    = integer2     not null with default,
    row_count   = integer2     not null with default) =
begin
end

field 'cusno' =
begin

/*
    If customer number has been entered on the screen, get the
    customer information.
*/

    customer = select *
    from customer
    where cusno = :cusno;

    inquire_ingres (row_count = rowcount,
            error_no = errorno);

    if (row_count = 0 or error_no != 0) then
     message 'Customer not found ...';
     sleep 2;
     clear field cusname, cusaddress, cuscity, cusstate, cuszip, cusphone;
    endif;

    resume next;
end

'Add' =
begin

/*
    Insert row.
*/

    insert into customer (*)
    values (customer.all);

    inquire_ingres (row_count = rowcount,
            error_no = errorno);

    if (row_count > 0 and error_no = 0) then
     message 'Customer added ...';
     sleep 2;

    elseif (row_count = 0 and error_no = 0) then
     message 'Customer was not added ...';
     sleep 2;

    elseif (error_no != 0) then
     message 'Problem adding customer ...';
```

FIGURE D.3 *continued*

```
     sleep 2;
   endif;

   resume field cusno;
end

'Update' =
begin

/*
   Update row.
*/

   update customer

   set cusname = :cusname,
     cusaddress = :cusaddress,
     cuscity = :cuscity,
     cusstate = :cusstate,
     cuszip = :cuszip,
     cusphone = :cusphone
   where cusno = :cusno;

   inquire_ingres (row_count = rowcount,
             error_no = errorno);

   if (row_count > 0 and error_no = 0) then
     message 'Customer updated ...';
     sleep 2;

   elseif (row_count = 0 and error_no = 0) then
     message 'Customer was not updated ...';
     sleep 2;

   elseif (error_no != 0) then
     message 'Problem updating customer ...';
     sleep 2;
   endif;

   resume field cusno;
end

'Delete' =
begin

/*
   Verify the delete.
*/

   answer = prompt 'Are you sure you want to delete this customer? (y/n)'
        with style = menuline;
   if (uppercase(answer) != 'Y') then
     resume field cusno;
   endif;

/*
   Delete row.
*/
```

```
    delete from customer
    where cusno = :cusno;

    inquire_ingres (row_count = rowcount,
            error_no = errorno);

    if (row_count > 0 and error_no = 0) then
     message 'Customer deleted ...';
     sleep 2;
     clear field all;

    elseif (row_count = 0 and error_no = 0) then
     message 'Customer was not deleted ...';
     sleep 2;

    elseif (error_no != 0) then
     message 'Problem deleting customer ...';
     sleep 2;
    endif;

    inquire_ingres (row_count = rowcount,
            error_no = errorno);

    resume field cusno;
end

'Find' =
begin

/*
    Provide help window.
*/

    callframe popcusname (cusno = byref(:cusno));

    customer =       select *
        from customer
        where cusno = :cusno;

    resume field cusname;
end

'Blank' =
begin

/*
    Blank all fields on the screen.
*/

    clear field all;
end

'Exit', key frskey3 =
begin

/*
    Return to topframe.
*/
    return;
end
```

FIGURE D.4 *Popcusname.OSQ*

```
/*
    Frame:   Popup customer name selection (popcusname.osq)
    Purpose: To display a window of customer names.  The selected
             customer's customer number is passed back to the
             calling program.
*/

initialize
    (row_count       = integer2 not null with default,
     cusno           = integer2 not null with default,
     error_no        = integer2 not null with default) =

begin

    inittable customer read;

    customer = select cusno,
                      cusname,
                      cusaddress,
                      cusphone
             from customer
             order by cusname;

/*
    If no rows were found, give message and return to calling program.
*/

    inquire_ingres (row_count = rowcount,
            error_no = errorno);

    if (row_count = 0 and error_no = 0) then
        message 'No rows found ...'
            with style = popup;
        return;
    endif;
end

'Select', key frskey4 =
begin

/*
    Select desired customer and return customer number.
*/

    cusno = :customer.cusno;
    return;
end

'Exit', key frskey3 =
begin
    return;
end
```

FIGURE D.5 *Inventory.OSQ*

```
/*
      Frame:   Maintain inventory information (inventory.osq)
      Purpose: To add, insert, and delete inventory information.
*/

initialize (
      answer                   = char(1)      not null with default,
      anychange                = integer2     not null with default,
      error_no                 = integer2     not null with default,
      inventorytbl.old_partno  = integer2     not null with default,
      inventorytbl.status      = integer2     not null with default,
      row_count                = integer2     not null with default,
      row_no                   = integer2     not null with default,
      state                    = integer1     not null with default) =

begin

/*
      Initialize tablefield and select into tablefield.   Since partno is
      the key to this table, select partno into a hidden column so that if
      the partno on the screen changes, the update will use the hidden
      column in the where clause.  Also use the hidden column 'status' to
      determine when a row has been inserted into the tablefield.
*/

      inittable inventorytbl fill;

      inventorytbl =
       select    partno,
            qty,
            itemname,
            reorder,
            cost,
            price,
            status = 2,
            old_partno = partno
        from inventory;
end

'Save' =
begin

      message 'Saving ...';
/*
      Set autocommit off to do transactions in MTS mode.
*/
      set autocommit off;

/*
      Remove rows marked for delete first.
*/

      unloadtable inventorytbl (state = _state)
      begin
       if (state = 4) then
            delete from inventory
            where partno = :inventorytbl.partno;
```

```
            inquire_ingres (error_no = errorno);
            if (error_no != 0) then
             rollback;
             commit;
             set autocommit on;
             message 'Problem updating rows ...';
             sleep 2;
             resume;
            endif;
      endif;
    end;

/*
    Do insert and update to rows.
*/

unloadtable inventorytbl (state = _state)
begin
 if (state = 1 or inventorytbl.status = 5) then
     insert into inventory (partno,
                    qty,
                    itemname,
                    reorder,
                    cost,
                        price)
     values (:inventorytbl.partno,
          :inventorytbl.qty,
          :inventorytbl.itemname,
          :inventorytbl.reorder,
          :inventorytbl.cost,
          :inventorytbl.price);

  elseif (state = 3 and inventorytbl.status != 5) then
     update inventory
     set partno    = :inventorytbl.partno,
      qty          = :inventorytbl.qty,
      itemname     = :inventorytbl.itemname,
      reorder      = :inventorytbl.reorder,
      cost         = :inventorytbl.cost,
      price        = :inventorytbl.price
     where partno  = :inventorytbl.old_partno;
  endif;

  inquire_ingres (error_no = errorno);
  if (error_no != 0) then
     rollback;
     commit;
     set autocommit on;
     message 'Problem updating rows ...';
     sleep 2;
     resume;
  endif;
end;

commit;

    set autocommit on;
```

FIGURE D.5 *continued*

```
/*
    Redisplay details.
*/

    inittable inventorytbl fill;

    inventorytbl =
     select    partno,
           qty,
           itemname,
           reorder,
           cost,
           price,
           status = 2,
           old_partno = partno
      from inventory;
/*
    Set the screen change flag to indicate changes have been saved.
*/

    set_forms form (change = 0);
    resume field inventorytbl;
end

'Delete' =
begin

/*
    Verify the delete.  If row is to be deleted from the tablefield,
    set the screen change flag.  The row will be deleted from the
    table  during the 'Save' processing.
*/

    answer = prompt 'Are you sure you want to delete this row? (y/n)'
     with style = menuline;
    if (uppercase(answer) = 'Y') then
     deleterow inventorytbl;

     set_forms form (change = 1);
    endif;
end

'Insert' =
begin

/*
    Insert row into tablefield.  Set row status to '5' to indicate this
    will be an insert.  */

    inquire_forms table '' (row_no = rowno);
    row_no = row_no - 1;
    insertrow inventorytbl[:row_no];
    inventorytbl.status = 5;
end
```

```
'Exit', key frskey3 =
begin

/*
    Determine if a row(s) have been deleted from table, rows updated, or
    rows added.  If change was found, make sure user wants to exit without
    saving.
*/

    inquire_forms form (anychange = change);
    if anychange = 1 then
     answer = prompt 'Changes are not saved.  Do you want to exit?'
         with style = menuline;
     if lowercase (left(answer, 1)) = 'y' then
         return;

     else
         resume;
     endif;
    endif;
    return;
end
```

FIGURE D.6 *Salespeople.OSQ*

```
/*
    Frame:   Maintain salespeople information (salespeople.osq)
    Purpose: To add, insert, and delete salespeople information.
*/

initialize (
    answer                    = char(1)      not null with default,
    anychange                 = integer2     not null with default,
    error_no                  = integer2     not null with default,
    salesmentbl.old_salesno   = integer2     not null with default,
    salesmentbl.status        = integer2     not null with default,
    row_count                 = integer2     not null with default,
    row_no                    = integer2     not null with default,
    state                     = integer1     not null with default) =

begin

/*
    Initialize tablefield and select into tablefield.   Since salesno is
    the key to this table, select salesno into a hidden column so that if
    the salesno on the screen changes, the update will use the hidden
    column in the where clause.  Also use the hidden column 'status' to
    determine when a row has been inserted into the tablefield.
*/

    inittable salespeopletbl fill;

    salespeopletbl =
     select     salesno,
          lname,
          fname,
          salesofc,
```

FIGURE D.6 *continued*

```
            status = 2,
            old_salesno = salesno
       from salespeople;

end

'Save' =
begin

    message 'Saving ...';
/*
    Set autocommit off to do transactions in MTS mode.
*/
    set autocommit off;

/*
    Remove rows marked for delete first.
*/

    unloadtable salespeopletbl (state = _state)
    begin
     if (state = 4) then
         delete from salespeople
         where salesno = :salespeopletbl.salesno;

         inquire_ingres (error_no = errorno);
         if (error_no != 0) then
          rollback;
          commit;
          set autocommit on;
          message 'Problem updating rows ...';
          sleep 2;
          resume;
         endif;
     endif;
    end;

/*
    Do insert and update to rows.
*/

    unloadtable salespeopletbl (state = _state)
    begin
    if (state = 1 or salespeopletbl.status = 5) then
        insert into salespeople (salesno,
                      lname,
                      fname,
                      salesofc)
        values (:salespeopletbl.salesno,
             :salespeopletbl.lname,
             :salespeopletbl.fname,
             :salespeopletbl.salesofc);

    elseif (state = 3 and salespeopletbl.status != 5) then
        update salesmen
        set salesno = :salespeopletbl.salesno,
         lname = :salespeopletbl.lname,
```

```
            fname = :salespeopletbl.fname,
            salesofc = :salespeopletbl.salesofc
          where salesno = :salespeopletbl.old_salesno;
     endif;

     inquire_ingres (error_no = errorno);
     if (error_no != 0) then
         rollback;
         commit;
         set autocommit on;
         message 'Problem updating rows ...';
         sleep 2;
         resume;
      endif;
    end;

    commit;
    set autocommit on;

/*
    Redisplay details.
*/

    inittable salespeopletbl fill;
    salespeopletbl =
     select     salesno,
          lname,
          fname,
          salesofc,
          status = 2,
          old_salesno = salesno
      from salespeople;
/*
    Set the screen change flag to indicate changes have been saved.
*/

    set_forms form (change = 0);
    resume field salespeopletbl;
end

'Delete' =
begin

/*
    Verify the delete.  If row is to be deleted from the tablefield,
    set the screen change flag.  The row will be deleted from the
    table  during the 'Save' processing.
*/

    answer = prompt 'Are you sure you want to delete this row? (y/n)'
     with style = menuline;
    if (uppercase(answer) = 'Y') then
     deleterow salespeopletbl;
     set_forms form (change = 1);
    endif;
end
```

```
'Insert' =
begin

/*
    Insert row into tablefield.  Set row status to '5' to indicate this
    will be an insert.

*/

    inquire_forms table '' (row_no = rowno);
    row_no = row_no - 1;
    insertrow salespeopletbl[:row_no];
    salespeopletbl.status = 5;
end

'Exit', key frskey3 =
begin

/*
    Determine if a row(s) have been deleted from table, rows updated, or
    rows added.  If change was found, make sure user wants to exit without
    saving.
*/

    inquire_forms form (anychange = change);
    if anychange = 1 then
     answer = prompt 'Changes are not saved.  Do you want to exit?'
         with style = menuline;
     if lowercase (left(answer, 1)) = 'y' then
         return;

     else
         resume;
     endif;
    endif;
    return;
end
```

LIST OF QUEL AND SQL COMMANDS WITH DATA TYPES AND FUNCTIONS

QUEL	SQL
----	---
ABORT	COMMIT
APPEND	COPY
BEGIN TRANSACTION	CREATE INDEX
COPY	CREATE INTEGRITY
CREATE	CREATE PROCEDURE
DEFINE INTEGRITY	CREATE TABLE
DEFINE PERMIT	CREATE VIEW
DEFINE VIEW	DELETE
DELETE	DROP
DESTROY	DROP INTEGRITY
DESTROY INTEGRITY	DROP PERMIT
DESTROY PERMIT	DROP PROCEDURE
END TRANSACTION	GRANT
HELP	HELP
INDEX	INSERT
MODIFY	MODIFY
PRINT	ROLLBACK
RANGE	SAVE
REPLACE	SAVEPOINT
RETRIEVE	SELECT
SAVE	SET
SAVEPOINT	UPDATE

```
QUEL data types:                        SQL data types:
----------------                        --------------
cn                                      char
text(n)                                 cn
i4                                      varchar(n)
i2                                      vchar(n)
i1                                      integer
f8                                      integer1
f4                                      integer2 (same as smallint)
date                                    integer4 (same as integer)
money                                   smallint
                                        float (same as float8)
                                        float4
                                        float8
                                        date
                                        money


QUEL set functions include:         SQL set functions:

COUNT(column_name)                  COUNT({[DISTINCT | ALL ] column_name} |*)
COUNTU(column_name)                 SUM([DISTINCT | ALL ]column_name)
SUM(column_name)                    AVG([DISTINCT | ALL ]column_name)
SUMU(column_name)                   MIN(column_name)
AVG(column_name)                    MAX(column_name)
AVGU(column_name)
MIN(column_name)
MAX(column_name)


QUEL Numeric functions include:        SQL Numeric functions include:

abs(n)                                  abs(n)
atan(n)                                 atan(n)
cos(n)                                  cos(n)
exp(n)                                  exp(n)
log(n)                                  log(n)
mod(n,b)                                mod(n,b)
sin(n)                                  sin(n)
sqrt(n)                                 sqrt(n)


QUEL type functions include:              SQL type functions include:

ascii(expr)                               ascii(expr)
date(expr)                                c(expr)
dow(expr)                                 char(expr)
float4(expr)                              date(expr)
float8(expr)                              dow(expr)
int2(expr)                                float4(expr)
int4(expr)                                float8(expr)
interval(x,y)                             hex(expr)
money(expr)                               int1(expr)
text(expr)                                int2(expr)
                                          int4(expr)
                                          interval(x,y)
                                          money(expr)
                                          varchar(expr)
                                          vchar(expr)
```

```
QUEL string_functions include:        SQL string functions include:

concat(string1,string2)               concat(string1,string2)
left(string1,length)                  left(string1,length)
length(string)                        length(string)
locate(string1,string2)               locate(string1,string2)
lowercase(string)                     lowercase(string)
pad(string)                           pad(string)
right(string,length)                  right(string,length)
shift(string,n_places)                shift(string,n_places)
size(string)                          size(string)
squeeze(string)                       squeeze(string)
money(expr)                           trim(string)
text(expr)                            Auppercase(string)
trim(string)                          charextract(c1,n)
uppercase(string)                     _date(s)
                                      _time(s)
```

Appendix F

ANSWERS TO SQL AND QUEL EXERCISES

1. Design exercises

a.
```
create table patients
     (first_name   c10,
      last_name    c15,
      address      c20,
      city         c15,
      state        c2,
      phone        c12,
      zip          c5,
      date_mem     date,
      cusid        i2);
commit;
```

b.
```
insert into patients
(first_name,last_name,address,city,state,phone,zip,date_mem,cusid)
values
('Sue','Gray','1212   W.   Thomas','Phoenix','AZ','602-943-8765',
     '85002','02-02-90',1001);
commit;

insert into patients
(first_name,last_name,address,city,state,phone,zip,date_mem,cusid)
values
('Harry','Ford','345 E. Northern','Phoenix','AZ','602-944-2366',
     '85610','01-10-90',1002);
commit;
```

```
insert into patients
(first_name,last_name,address,city,state,phone,zip,date_mem,cusid)
values
('George','Burns','111 N. 13th Ave.','Tucson','AZ','602-345-3210',
    '85122','03-09-90',1003);
commit;

insert into patients
(first_name,last_name,address,city,state,phone,zip,date_mem,cusid)
values
('Sherns','Adams','4532 W. Indian','Tucson','AZ','602-465-2349',
    '85122','03-11-90',1004);
commit;

insert into patients
(first_name,last_name,address,city,state,phone,zip,date_mem,cusid)
values
('Ann','Wilson','7538 N. Central','Phoenix','AZ','602-945-8877',
    '85334','04-11-90',1005);
commit;

insert into patients
(first_name,last_name,address,city,state,phone,zip,date_mem,cusid)
values
('Majid','Rezai','4500 E. Rasht','Chandler','AZ','602-555-6678',
    '85444','01-05-90',1006);
commit;


c.
create table fees
    (cusid        i2,
    fees          money,
    date_billed   date);
commit;


d.
insert into fees
(cusid,fees,date_billed)
values
(1001,55.50,'03-10-90');
commit;

insert into fees
(cusid,fees,date_billed)
values
(1003,75.00,'07-10-90');
commit;

insert into fees
(cusid,fees,date_billed)
values
(1006,100.00,'01-01-90');
commit;

insert into fees
(cusid,fees,date_billed)
values
(1002,43.00,'02-02-90');
commit;
```

```
insert into fees
(cusid,fees,date_billed)
values
(1004,67.50,'10-10-90');
commit;

insert into fees
(cusid,fees,date_billed)
values
(1005,73.00,'5-12-90');
commit;

insert into fees
(cusid,fees,date_billed)
values
(1006,67.50,'10-10-90');
commit;

insert into fees
(cusid,fees,date_billed)
values
(1001,35.00,'10-10-90');
commit;

insert into fees
(cusid,fees,date_billed)
values
(1002,25.00,'03-02-90');
commit;

insert into fees
(cusid,fees,date_billed)
values
(1006,25.00,'10-31-90');
commit;

insert into fees
(cusid,fees,date_billed)
values
(1003,35.00,'08-10-90');
commit;

insert into fees
(cusid,fees,date_billed)
values
(1001,89.00,'05-01-90');
commit;


e.
create table feespaid
      (cusid      i2,
      fees_paid   money,
      date_paid   date);
commit;


f.
insert into feespaid
(cusid,fees_paid,date_paid)
```

```
values
(1001,55.50,'04-10-90');
commit;

insert into feespaid
(cusid,fees_paid,date_paid)
values
(1002,43.00,'03-03-90');
commit;

insert into feespaid
(cusid,fees_paid,date_paid)
values
(1006,100.00,'02-01-90');
commit;

insert into feespaid
(cusid,fees_paid,date_paid)
values
(1003,35.00,'09-15-90');
commit;

insert into feespaid
(cusid,fees_paid,date_paid)
values
(1001,89.00,'06-01-90');
commit;

insert into feespaid
(cusid,fees_paid,date_paid)
values
(1001,35.00,'10-15-90');
commit;

insert into feespaid
(cusid,fees_paid,date_paid)
values
(1002,25.00,'04-02-90');
commit;

insert into feespaid
(cusid,fees_paid,date_paid)
values
(1003,35.00,'08-10-90');
commit;

insert into feespaid
(cusid,fees_paid,date_paid)
values
(1005,73.00,'6-12-90');
commit;

insert into feespaid
(cusid,fees_paid,date_paid)
values
(1006,67.50,'10-15-90');
commit;

insert into feespaid
(cusid,fees_paid,date_paid)
```

```
values
(1006,25.00,'11-01-90');
commit;


2.  SQL  Select statement exercises

a.
select *
from patients;
commit;

b.
select last_name,address
from patients;
commit;

c.
select *
from patients
where city = 'Tucson';
commit;

d.
select *
from patients
where date_mem >= '01-12-90'
and date_mem   <= '06-10-90';
commit;

e.
select first_name
from patients
order by first_name;
commit;

f.
select patients.first_name,fees.cusid,fees.date_billed
from patients,fees
where patients.cusid=fees.cusid
and fees.date_billed <= '10-10-90';
commit;

g.
select patients.city,patients.state,patients.first_name,
patients.last_name,fees.fees
from patients,fees
where patients.cusid=fees.cusid
and fees.fees >= 75.00;
commit;

h.
select first_name,cusid
from patients
where cusid >= 1002
and cusid <= 1005;
commit;
```

```
i.
select distinct
patients.first_name,patients.last_name,patients.cusid,
     fees.date_billed,fees.fees
from patients,fees
where patients.cusid=fees.cusid
and not exists
     (select feespaid.*
     from feespaid
     where feespaid.cusid=patients.cusid);
commit;

j.
select *
from fees;
commit;

k.
select *
from feespaid;
commit;

l.
select patients.*,fees.*
from fees,patients
where patients.cusid=fees.cusid;
commit;

m.
select distinct patients.city,patients.state,patients.first_name,
     patients.last_name,fees.fees
from patients,fees
where fees.fees >= 20.00
and fees.fees <= 100.00
and patients.cusid=fees.cusid;
commit;

n.
select patients.*,fees.fees
from patients,fees
where patients.city='Phoenix'
and patients.cusid=fees.cusid;
commit;

o.
select patients.cusid,patients.first_name,patients.last_name
from patients;
commit;
```

Chapter Five   SQL Aggregate Operators

1. Aggregates exercises

```
a.
select Total=sum(fees.fees),fees.cusid,patients.first_name,
     patients.last_name
```

```
from fees,patients
where fees.cusid=patients.cusid
group by fees.cusid,patients.first_name,patients.last_name;
commit;
```

b.
```
select    Total=sum(feespaid.fees_paid),patients.first_name,
     patients.address
from feespaid,patients
where feespaid.cusid=patients.cusid
group by feespaid.fees_paid,patients.first_name,patients.address;
commit;
```

c.
```
select MaxFee=max(fees.fees),patients.first_name,patients.cusid
from fees,patients
where fees.cusid=patients.cusid
group by patients.first_name,patients.cusid;
commit;
```

d.
```
select    MinFee=min(fees.fees),patients.first_name,
     patients.last_name, patients.cusid
from fees,patients
where fees.cusid=patients.cusid
group by patients.first_name,patients.last_name,patients.cusid;
commit;
```

e.
```
select AvgFee=avg(fees.fees),patients.cusid,patients.last_name
from fees,patients
where fees.cusid=patients.cusid
group by patients.cusid,patients.last_name;
commit;
```

f.
```
select    distinct    patients.first_name,patients.last_name,
     Total=sum(fees.fees)
from patients,fees
where patients.cusid=fees.cusid
and not exists
     (select feespaid.*
     from feespaid
     where feespaid.cusid=patients.cusid)
group by patients.first_name,patients.last_name;
commit;
```

2. INSERT, UPDATE, and DELETE exercises

a.
```
insert into patients
(first_name,last_name,address,city,state,phone,zip,date_mem,cusid)
values
('Arther','Simson','1200  W.  Kearn','Yuma','AZ','602-859-2299',
'85400','05-05-90',1007);
commit;
```

b.
```
insert into fees
```

```
(cusid,fees,date_billed)
values
(1007,66.00,'06-06-90');
commit;

c.
update fees
set fees = 73.00
where fees.cusid=1005;
commit;

d.
insert into feespaid
(cusid,fees_paid,date_paid)
values
(1003,40.00,'11-01-90');
commit;

e.
select    patients.first_name,patients.last_name,patients.cusid,
fees.fees,TotalPaid=sum(feespaid.fees_paid)
from patients,fees,feespaid
where patients.cusid=1003
and patients.cusid=fees.cusid
and fees.cusid=feespaid.cusid
group  by  patients.first_name,patients.last_name,patients.cusid,
fees.fees;
commit;

f.
insert into patients
(first_name,last_name,address,city,state,phone,zip,date_mem,cusid)
values
('Esmat','Asghari','7501 E. Palo Verde Dr.','Scottsdale','AZ',
     '602-483-7921','85250','09-10-90',1008);
commit;

g.
insert into fees
(cusid,fees,date_billed)
values
(1008,75.00,'10-10-90');
commit;

h.
insert into fees
(cusid,fees,date_billed)
values
(1008,50.00,'10-15-90');
commit;

i.
select patients.first_name,patients.last_name,patients.cusid,
     Total=sum(fees.fees)
from patients,fees
where fees.cusid=1008
and patients.cusid=fees.cusid
group by patients.first_name,patients.last_name,patients.cusid;
commit;
```

```
j.
select Total=sum(fees.fees)
from fees;
commit;
```

Chapter Six QUEL exercises

1. Design exercises

a.
```
create patients
      (first_name = char(10),
       last_name  = char(15),
       address    = char(20),
       city       = char(15),
       state      = char(2),
       phone      = char(12),
       zip        = char(5),
       date_mem   = date,
       cusid      = i2)
```

b.
```
append to patients
(first_name = "Sue", last_name = "Gary", address = "1212 W.
Thomas",city = "Phoenix", state = "AZ", phone = "602-943-8765", zip
= "85002",date_mem = "02-01-90", cusid = 1001)

append to patients
(first_name = "Harry", last_name = "Ford", address = "345 E.
Northern",city = "Phoenix", state = "AZ", phone = "602-944-2366",
zip = "85349",date_mem = "01-10-90", cusid = 1002)

append to patients
(first_name = "George", last_name = "Burns", address = "111 N. 13th
Ave.",city = "Tucson", state = "AZ", phone = "602-345-3210", zip =
"85610",date_mem = "03-09-90", cusid = 1003)

append to patients
(first_name = "Sherns", last_name = "Adams", address = "4532 W.
Indian",city = "Tucson", state = "AZ", phone = "602-465-2349", zip
= "85122",date_mem = "03-11-90", cusid = 1004)

append to patients
(first_name = "Ann", last_name = "Wilson", address = "7538 N.
Central",city = "Phoenix", state = "AZ", phone = "602-945-8877",
zip = "85334",date_mem = "04-11-90", cusid = 1005)

append to patients
(first_name = "Majid", last_name = "Rezai", address = "4500 E.
Rasht", city = "Chandler", state = "AZ", phone = "602-555-6678",
zip = "85444",date_mem = "01-05-90", cusid = 1006)
```

c.
```
create fees
      (cusid       = i2,
       fees        = money,
       date_billed = date)
```

d.
```
append to fees
(cusid = 1001, fees = 55.50, date_billed = "03-10-90")

append to fees
(cusid = 1003, fees = 75.00, date_billed = "07-10-90")

append to fees
(cusid = 1006, fees = 100.00, date_billed = "01-10-90")

append to fees
(cusid = 1002, fees = 43.00, date_billed = "02-02-90")

append to fees
(cusid = 1004, fees = 67.50, date_billed = "10-10-90")

append to fees
(cusid = 1005, fees = 80.00, date_billed = "12-12-90")

append to fees
(cusid = 1006, fees = 75.00, date_billed = "05-10-90")

append to fees
(cusid = 1001, fees = 89.00, date_billed = "05-10-90")
```

e.
```
create feespaid
     (cusid     = i2,
     fees_paid = money,
     date_paid = date)
```

f.
```
append to feespaid
(cusid = 1004, fees_paid = 67.50, date_paid = "11-11-90")

append to feespaid
(cusid = 1001, fees_paid = 55.50, date_paid = "03-10-90")

append to feespaid
(cusid = 1002, fees_paid = 43.00, date_paid = "04-02-90")

append to feespaid
(cusid = 1006, fees_paid = 100.00, date_paid = "02-01-90")

append to feespaid
(cusid = 1003, fees_paid = 35.00, date_paid = "08-10-90")

append to feespaid
(cusid = 1001, fees_paid = 90.00, date_paid = "05-01-90")
```

2.   **Retrieve** statement exercises

a.
```
retrieve (patients.all)
```

```
b.
retrieve (patients.last_name,patients.address)

c.
retrieve (patients.all)
where patients.city = "Tucson"

d.
retrieve (patients.all)
where patients.date_mem >= "01-12-90"
and patients.date_mem <= "06-10-90"

e.
retrieve (patients.first_name)
sort by first_name

f.
retrieve (patients.first_name,fees.cusid,fees.date_billed)
where patients.cusid=fees.cusid
and fees.date_billed <= "10-10-90"

g.
retrieve (patients.city, patients.state, patients.first_name,
     patients.last_name)
where patients.cusid=fees.cusid
and fees.fees >= 75.00

h.
retrieve (patients.first_name,patients.cusid)
where patients.cusid >= 1002
and patients.cusid <= 1005

i.
retrieve (fees.all)

j.
retrieve (feespaid.all)

k.
retrieve (patients.all,fees.all)
where patients.cusid=fees.cusid

l)
retrieve    (patients.city,patients.state,patients.first_name,
     patients.last_name)
where fees.fees >= 20.00
and fees.fees <= 100.00

m.
retrieve (patients.all,fees.fees)
where patients.city='Phoenix'
and patients.cusid=fees.cusid

n.
retrieve (patients.cusid,patients.first_name,patients.last_name)
```

Appendix G

ADVANCED SQL PROGRAMMING

At this point we have learned how to create tables and insert data in SQl into a database. We can do all of this in one program and let SQL create the table and insert the data for us.

Create the following program in your editor and name it **sqlprog.sql.**

FIGURE G.1 *Sqlprog.sql*

```
/*
    Author:
    Purpose: The following program will create the tables, and
             insert the data into the table.
*/


/* Creating a table called DEMOSALES */
/************************************/

create table demosales
     /* Assigning and specifying columns into the table */

     (lname c25,
     fname c15,
     salesno smallint,
     salesofc c25);
commit;
\g

    /* Inserting data into the assigned and specified columns */

    insert into demosales
         (lname,fname,salesno,salesofc)
             values ('Johnson','Henry',1001,'Phoenix');
    commit;
    \g
```

FIGURE G.1 *continued*

```
insert into demosales
     (lname,fname,salesno,salesofc)
          values ('Castro','Robert',1002,'Phoenix');
commit;
\g

insert into demosales
     (lname,fname,salesno,salesofc)
          values ('Barton','Jane',1003,'Phoenix');
commit;
\g

insert into demosales
     (lname,fname,salesno,salesofc)
          values ('Smith','John',2001,'Las Vegas');
commit;
\g

insert into demosales
     (lname,fname,salesno,salesofc)
          values ('Santos','Clarissa',3001,'San Diego');
commit;
\g

insert into demosales
     (lname,fname,salesno,salesofc)
          values ('Travis','Randy',4001,'El Paso');
commit;
\g


/* Display the table, DEMOSALES, with its data.
        Also to make sure Ingres (SQL) created the results
               that we requested. */
select *          /* Select all the columns */
from demosales; /* From table_name */
commit;
\g               /* Execute command GO for SQL */

/* Create a table called DEMOINV */

create table demoinv
     /* Assigning and specifying the columns for the table */

    (partno smallint,
    qty smallint,
    description c30,
    reorder smallint,
    cost money,
    price money);
    commit;
    \g

    /* Inserting data into the assigned and specified columns */

    insert into demoinv
         (partno,qty,description,reorder,cost,price)
              values (9111,2000,'Wrench',100,1.35,1.95);
```

```
     commit;
     \g

     insert into demoinv
           (partno,qty,description,reorder,cost,price)
                 values (9112,100,'Socket set',20,14.95,21.70);
     commit;
     \g

     insert into demoinv
           (partno,qty,description,reorder,cost,price)
                 values (9113,250,'Srewdriver, #2',50,0.89,1.30);
     commit;
     \g

     insert into demoinv
           (partno,qty,description,reorder,cost,price)
                 values (9114,60,'Test meter, M5',10,25.50,36.99);
     commit;
     \g

     insert into demoinv
           (partno,qty,description,reorder,cost,price)
                 values (9115,3500,'Pliers, 3 inch',200,1.50,2.18);

     commit;
     \g


     /* Display the table, DEMOINV, with its data. Also to
           make sure Ingres (SQL) has created the results that we
           requested. */


select *        /* Select all the columns */
from demoinv;   /* From table_name */
commit;
\g              /* Execute command Go */


/* Creating a table called DEMOCUS */

create table democus
            /* Assigning and specifying columns into the table */

     (cusname c25,
     cusaddress c25,
     cuscity c25,
     cusstate c2,
     cuszip c5,
     cusphone c12,
     cusno smallint);
     commit;
     \g
    /* Inserting data into the assigned and specified columns */


insert into democus
(cusname,cusaddress,cuscity,cusstate,cuszip,cusphone,cusno)
                values
```

```
('Arizona Suppy','65 S. Central','Phoenix','Az','85012',
'602-271-4955',8113);
commit;
\g

insert into democus
(cusname,cusaddress,cuscity,cusstate,cuszip,cusphone,cusno)
                values
('Atlas Supply','1234 W. Thomas','Phoenix','Az','85019',
'602-235-4311',8111);
commit;
\g

insert into democus
(cusname,cusaddress,cuscity,cusstate,cuszip,cusphone,cusno)
                values
('Desert Vendors','33. N. Outerloop','Las Vegas','Nv','71345',
'215-333-4111',8114);
commit;
\g

insert into democus
(cusname,cusaddress,cuscity,cusstate,cuszip,cusphone,cusno)
                values
('Ocean Supply','65 Marine Way','San Diego','Ca','24035',
'591-695-2211',8116);
commit;
\g

insert into democus
(cusname,cusaddress,cuscity,cusstate,cuszip,cusphone,cusno)
                values
('Saguaro Wholesale','351 Highland','Phoenix','Az','85001',
'602-344-6000',8112);
commit;
\g

insert into democus
(cusname,cusaddress,cuscity,cusstate,cuszip,cusphone,cusno)
                values
('Western Wholesale','2501 Lee Trevino','El Paso','Tx','64311',
'415-222-6111',8115);
commit;
\g


   /* Display the table, DEMOCUS, with its data.
      Also to make sure Ingres (SQL) created the results that we
      requested. */


select *        /* Select all the columns */
from democus;   /* From the table_name */
commit;
\g              /* Execute command GO */


/* Create a table called DEMOTRAN */
```

```
create table demotran
        /* Assigning and specifying the columns for the table */

    (salesno smallint,
    cusno smallint,
    partno smallint,
    date date,
    deldate date,
    qty smallint,
    orderprice money);
    commit;
    \g

    /* Inserting data into the assigned and specified columns */


insert into demotran
(salesno,cusno,partno,date,deldate,qty,orderprice)
                values
(1001,8111,9111,'02-20-1989','03-15-1989',5,9.75);
commit;
\g

insert into demotran
(salesno,cusno,partno,date,deldate,qty,orderprice)
                values
(0,8113,9114,'02-18-1989','02-28-1989',1,36.99);
commit;
\g

insert into demotran
(salesno,cusno,partno,date,deldate,qty,orderprice)
                values
(1002,8113,9113,'01-30-1989','02-28-1989',10,13.00);
commit;
\g

insert into demotran
(salesno,cusno,partno,date,deldate,qty,orderprice)
                values
(1003,8112,9112,'02-15-1989','03-01-1989',3,65.10);
commit;
\g

insert into demotran
(salesno,cusno,partno,date,deldate,qty,orderprice)
                values
(2001,8114,9115,'01-31-1989','02-28-1989',5,10.90);
commit;
\g

insert into demotran
(salesno,cusno,partno,date,deldate,qty,orderprice)
                values
(3001,8116,9111,'02-10-1989','03-15-1989',15,29.25);
commit;
\g
```

FIGURE G.1 *continued*

```
insert into demotran
(salesno,cusno,partno,date,deldate,qty,orderprice)
                values
(4001,8115,9114,'02-05-1989','02-28-1989',2,73.98);
commit;
\g

    /* Display the table, DEMOTRAN, with its data. Also
       to make sure Ingres (SQL) created the results that we
       requested. */


select *            /* Select all the columns */
from demotran;      /* From the table_name */
commit;
\g                  /* execute command GO */

\date,\time         /* Print the date and the time */

\q                  /* To quit Ingres (SQL) */
```

To get into SQL commandline, type:

   sql <database_name>

At the SQL prompt type:

   \i sqlprog.sql

The '\i' allows SQL to insert a file into the command line and execute it. You will see SQL executing all the lines in sequence order.

INDEX

J